TEACHING STUDENTS WAYS TO REMEMBER

Strategies for Learning Mnemonically

MARGO A. MASTROPIERI
THOMAS E. SCRUGGS

Purdue University

A volume in the series on Cognitive Strategy Instruction
Series Editor: Michael Pressley

Brookline Books

Library of Congress Cataloging-in-Publication Data

Mastropieri, Margo A., 1951 -
    Teaching students ways to remember: strategies for learning
    mnemonically / Margo A. Mastropieri, Thomas E. Scruggs.
            p.   cm.
    Includes bibliographical references (p.   ), index.
    ISBN 0-914797-67-0
    1. Mnemonics. 2. Study, Method of.   I. Scruggs, Thomas E.,
    1948 - . II. Title.
    LB1063. M28   1991
    371.3—dc20

                                              91-3904
                                              CIP

Published by
Brookline Books
P.O. Box 1046, Cambridge, MA 02238-1046

Acknowledgements

We would like to thank the teachers, administrators, and students from schools in Massachusetts, Arizona, Utah, Wisconsin, and Indiana who influenced our thinking and generously cooperated with our projects. Although the entire list of persons to whom we are indebted is too lengthy to provide here, we would like to express particular thanks to Dr. Hal McGrady, the teachers of the Mesa, Arizona Public Schools, Dr. Barbara McLoone, Ann Marie Domek and Judy Little, and Cecilia Mimms of Indianapolis Public Schools, and undergraduate and graduate students and staff who have worked with us over the past decade, including Dr. Debra Tolfa Veit, Dr. Barbara Fulk, Dr. Richard Laufenberg, Sister Sharon Sullivan, Frederick Brigham, Jeff Bakken, Sharlene Shiah, Sue Hesser, Terri Milham, Lori Baker Jones, Kara Chenoweth, Cheryl DeLuca, Shanna Weagle, Sarah Lamb, Robyn Kipnis, Mary Ellen Heiner, and Debra Peck. Finally, we would like to thank our parents, Francis and Dorothy Mastropieri, and Edward B. and Janet H. Scruggs, for their unfailing support throughout our lives.

Table of Contents

List of Figures

PREFACE

Mnemonics and Teaching

As shown in the picture, a "mnemonic" is a technique or device for improving or strengthening memory. In this picture, a *demonic* figure is providing a *demonic mnemonic* so that the former offender won't forget his offenses. This link helps you remember the meaning of "mnemonic".

We began conducting research on mnemonic instruction in 1982. After a decade of applied research, involving over 1,000 students, we have shown mnemonic instruction to dramatically improve school success, especially for students with learning problems. Over the years, we have presented these data on the effectiveness of mnemonic instruction at school districts, universities, and meetings of state and national professional educational organizations, and discovered an enormous interest in mnemonic instruction by teachers and administrators. This book was written in response to those requesting additional information on how mnemonic instruction can be used with their particular students.

It is difficult to overstate the importance of a well-developed

FIgure P.l Mnemonic (demonic) = A Method for Improving Memory

memory. It is not enough to say "they can always look it up in an encyclopedia"; one needs a sufficient knowledge base to know *what* to look up. Research has shown that students who have the most firmly established knowledge base are the ones who can most easily assimilate and apply new information. This phenomenon has been dubbed the "Matthew Effect," whereby the informationally "rich" become richer and the informationally poor become poorer. The best way to break this cycle is to find a means for promoting the acquisition of a firm and thorough knowledge base in all students. Mnemonic instruction is uniquely suited for this purpose.

This manual emphasizes the use of mnemonic techniques to foster a student's memory. Clearly the techniques we describe should not be used exclusively in a class. We do recommend in the final chapter that teachers should remind students to use these techniques when the students are trying to remember materials they have learned as part of the larger lessons you are engaged in. These techniques will only be embraced by students when they see they help them learn, know, remember, and can recall what they have learned. For this to happen, teachers must remind students to use them, perhaps review the relevant techniques to use orally, and reinforce and support their use as much as they can.

But these activities should be seen as supplementary to the other learning activities in school. Learning is a complex, not a unitary, process. Students need background knowledge for experiences to be meaningful. Imagine taking a group of children on a field trip to view a Gutenberg Bible. What meaning could such a trip have for students who lack knowledge of the history of the printing press and the enormous changes it brought to Western civilization?

Effective teachers need to promote all aspects of the learning process. This book focuses on techniques which help students acquire basic skills, concepts, facts, and systems of facts—what mnemonic instruction facilitates most. However, this should not be taken to mean that we do not recommend promoting creativity, critical thinking, evaluation, and problem solving. In fact, the use of mnemonic techniques helps basic information to be mastered so readily that more time will be available for these "higher order" skills and experiences!

How to Use This Book

Section 1 of this book explains several major mnemonic techniques, how to do them, and what applications they are best suited for. Section 2 provides examples of applications to various areas in the curriculum—social studies, science, mathematics and other basic skills. These chapters indicate the mnemonic techniques that can be used and the tasks they are suitable for within these areas, provide examples of the use of these techniques using applications within the curriculum area, and ends with a sample lesson for you to review.

We used as many examples as possible, for the best way to learn about mnemonic instruction is to present examples and how to solve them. As you go through the applications chapters in Section 2 there are some exercises for you to do on your own, with our choices at the end of the chapter. But before you turn to our choices, try hard to develop your own using a mnemonic technique and test their effectiveness. These activities will show you how easily you can learn how to adapt content to mnemonic instruction, and how easily you can figure out how to use these techniques even when they seem difficult to apply to a particular situation.

When you adapt classroom information so your students can use mnemonic techniques, first identify the most important content you wish to teach, without concern for the level of difficulty involved in developing mnemonic strategies. Next, develop mnemonic strategies using the techniques described in this book. At this point in the process it helps to do a lot of brainstorming; with more than one person you can generate a lot of possibilities. Do this, at first, without evaluating alternative choices. After you generate a number of alternatives, select the best ones. If none seem adequate, put that item aside for the moment and turn to the next item to be adapted. Finally, consider any items for which you could not develop an effective mnemonic option: usually in a day or so effective choices will come to you. Don't give up: persistence usually results in success, and some choices which seem weak or less than adequate can still be more effective than no strategy at all. It is also true that you will become more efficient at developing these choices as you gain more experience. When you see for yourself how well these mnemonic techniques work, you will become as enthusiastic as we are about mnemonic instruction!

Section One

Some Mnemonic Techniques

CHAPTER 1

What are Mnemonics? Most Frequently Asked Questions

Many mnemonic techniques, and the overall purposes of mnemonic instruction, are not familiar to most people. In order to help you understand what mnemonic instruction involves, this chapter lists questions most commonly asked about mnemonic instruction. These questions and answers are intended to provide you with an overview of mnemonic instruction, and to encourage you to read on to learn how you can apply these effective techniques in your classroom.

1. What is mnemonic instruction? Mnemonic instruction is a technique for increasing the initial learning and long-term retention of important information. Using mnemonic instructional techniques, teachers typically present not only important information, but also effective *strategies* for learning and later retrieval of this information. Usually, these strategies take the form of pictures (or mental "images") which contain both representations of the information and a concrete link to the student's own knowledge system.

Mnemonic techniques were well known to the ancient Greeks, who, without easy access to writing and written material, were compelled to develop strong memory skills in order to remember what they had heard. According to legend, mnemonics were developed by an ancient orator named Simonides. Simonides was invited to the house of a wealthy nobleman to recite a poem dedicated to him in the presence of his dinner guests. Simonides delivered this oration honoring the nobleman, but afterwards, while Simonides was outside the building, the roof caved in, mutilating the bodies of the guests so badly that their relatives could not identify them. Simonides was able to identify all the guests because he had remembered the image of the *places* the guests had occupied. This incident gave Simonides an insight that mental imagery can be very useful in the development of memory skills. He began to develop a system of mnemonics which was widely used in ancient times.

Some of these ancient memory techniques survived through the Middle Ages, sometimes associated with magic and the occult, as with the mysterious "memory theatre" of Giulio Camillo, or Giordano Bruno and his secret of "Shadows." After the invention and development of the printing press, however, the art of memory began to decline in importance.

Throughout the twentieth century, interest in mnemonics has increased. Most recently, in 1975, Richard Atkinson described an approach, previously described by the Greeks, he called the "keyword method." He showed the effectiveness of this method in teaching Russian vocabulary. A very large number of research studies since validated and extended his work to other applications. Only very recently have mnemonics been used as classroom teaching and learning techniques, mostly in our own projects.

2. How effective is mnemonic instruction? In a large number of experimental research studies conducted during the past decade (see Mastropieri & Scruggs, 1989, for a review), students who received mnemonic instruction greatly outperformed controls taught by traditional instructional techniques. In classroom applications of these techniques, student performance has more than doubled on content tests and average grades have improved from "D+" to "B"! In addition, teachers using mnemonic instruction reported that this type of instruction was especially suited for children who often have difficulty learning. Mnemonic instruction also improved attitudes toward school and promoted more positive classroom interaction on the part of their students. Certainly, mnemonic instruction has the power to make major positive changes in the classroom.

3. What can be taught using mnemonic instruction? Most previous research has been conducted in the areas of English and foreign language vocabulary, science, history, geography, and social studies. However, mnemonic instruction has also been shown to improve mathematics, phonics, and spelling. Mnemonic instruction is helpful whenever there is important information to remember.

4. Since mnemonic instruction relies so heavily on pictures, can students who are primarily "auditory learners" benefit from them as well as students who are "visual learners?" We have never found a "type of learner" who could not benefit from mnemonic instruction except in the rare case of the student who already applies these strategies to his or her own learning. However, it is important to note that mnemonic instruction utilizes pictured images as well as specific verbal elaboration. If there is such a thing as an "auditory learner" who can not learn from a picture (if, in fact, such cases can be easily identified), there are ample auditory cues within the verbal elaborations to help such students.

5. I am not artistically inclined. How can I develop the pictures necessary for mnemonic instruction? There are several possibilities for the teacher who does not feel particularly artistic. These are listed below:

a. Research has shown that mnemonic pictures do not have to be artistic to be effective. Any picture which is recognizable is helpful for mnemonic instruction.

b. Teachers who cannot draw at all can develop mnemonic pictures using cutouts from magazines and stick figures. One of the teachers we worked with used exactly this method, and was very successful.

c. Most schools have students enrolled in art classes who can produce cartoon like illustrations. It may be possible to enlist the aid of these artistically inclined students to draw mnemonic pictures.

d. If producing pictures proves to be altogether impossible, teachers can promote *visual imagery* in their students. The teacher describes the picture and asks all students to form their own mental picture. Through repeated questioning of the students regarding details of the image (regarding, e.g., where characters are standing or sitting, position, size, etc.), a strong visual image is formed. Although not as powerful as pictures, visual images nonetheless can also be very effective.

6. With all the paper work and other demands on my time, I simply don't have time to develop mnemonic strategies and pictures for everything I teach. When am I supposed to find the time to do this? There is no doubt that developing mnemonic teaching techniques can be time-consuming (and sometimes frustrating) to develop. However, our firm position is that developing mnemonic teaching techniques can, in the long run, *save* you time. Keep in mind that most teachers teach the same or similar content year after year. Mnemonic materials, once developed, can be used again and again. Mnemonic instruction can substantially *reduce* the time required for teaching the content, potentially freeing you for other activities.

At first, use just a few techniques so you can become familiar with them and you and your students can start to think "mnemonically." As you become comfortable and more experienced in thinking about how to incorporate mnemonic techniques in your teaching, you can add both additional techniques and expand the areas in which you are applying them. This will help you and your students. As you use techniques they are familiar with in new areas of the curriculum, they see how effective the same techniques they have already learned and used can be for them. They become more adept at applying the technique but they may also use the technique in more and more situations *themselves*, because they see its power to help them learn and remember.

We discuss how to help students learn to use mnemonic techniques on their own, *independently*, in the last chapter. Once you have become convinced of the utility and effectiveness of these techniques, it becomes the most important task of all since we want our students to function as independent learners.

7. After too many of these mnemonic pictures, don't students become confused? This concern arises in part because mnemonics attempts to improve memory by *adding to*, rather than subtracting the amount of information to be remembered. However, research has shown that the brain's ultimate capacity for storage of new information is virtually limitless. But when retrieval routes are lost, as is the case in much traditional instruction, students can become easily overloaded with information and suffer confusion. Teachers must always be aware of the optimal amount of information they can present in one lesson; however, more information will be remembered if it is presented mnemonically.

8. How many mnemonic pictures should I present in one lesson? How much new information should be presented depends, of course, on the difficulty of the content, the age and ability level of the students, and to a certain extent, your skills and comfort as a teacher to present materials mnemonically. In our classroom studies, teachers rarely presented more than 6 to 8 pictures in an individual lesson. Time must also be allocated to review previous lessons, and for the class to discuss previous and present content. However, if only a list of highly related information is being taught (e.g., vocabulary words, states and capitals, mineral hardness levels), and the mnemonic techniques are similar, it may be possible to teach more than 6-8 items. In one experiment with difficult-to-teach students, students were shown 26 different mnemonic pictures in one thirty-minute lesson, and remembered most of them. However, this amount of mnemonic instruction in so short a time was done for experimental purposes only; ordinarily far less content is recommended for classroom teaching.

9. Why can't students simply be taught to develop their own mnemonic strategies without me doing it for them? Students can be taught to use these strategies independently, and the final chapter in this book is devoted to a discussion of how this can be done. However, many students most likely will be less efficient at developing strategies than their teachers. When content learning has the highest priority, teachers should help develop learning and memory strategies. When independent study skills are being taught, and are, at the time, considered of more importance than the content at hand, independent strategy use should be taught. Since these are complex strategies, however, students who have been taught mnemonically over extended periods of time will be most likely to transfer use of the strategies to their own learning.

10. I think there are more important things to do in school than simply to memorize facts. Aren't you simply proposing a more efficient way of doing something that already gets far more attention than it deserves? There are many important things to learn and do in school, and learning and retaining factual information is only one component of the entire school experience. However, it is our contention that a strong declarative knowledge base is an absolutely critical first step to such "higher level" skills as critical thinking and problem solving. This is particularly true for students who do not have a strong knowledge base.

It is important to note that one must first *remember* important information before one can think critically or solve problems with it. For instance, imagine conducting a "critical" discussion of current events with a group of students who have no relevant information about current events. Or, imagine discussing the relationship between the Thirty Years' War and the Pilgrims' departure for the New World with a group of students who do not know or remember when or where either event occurred, or even what the events were. In much of the contemporary discussion of the importance of higher level thinking skills, the fact that students must have first acquired an adequate knowledge base to have something to think *about*, has sometimes been ignored.

SUMMARY

Unlike many other techniques, mnemonic instruction not only helps students to acquire new information and it helps them remember it. It can be used in any area, from mathematics to history to vocabulary to spelling. It is an instrument that allows the student to learn and remember new information quickly and easily. It has been shown to enhance comprehension and heighten motivation and enthusiasm for school learning. Once you learn to apply the techniques described in this book, we are certain you will appreciate the enormous classroom potential of mnemonic instruction.

CHAPTER 2

Mnemonic Vocabulary Instruction: Using the Keyword Method

Vocabulary learning is critically important for success in school. Research has shown that a strong vocabulary is positively related to such tasks as reading, listening comprehension, and good conversational skills. Many students are unable to achieve up to their potential in school, not because they are "stupid" or "lazy," but simply because they do not understand much of the vocabulary they read or hear. This chapter describes in detail how to enhance vocabulary knowledge using the *keyword method*. The keyword method has also been applied to a variety of other learning tasks; these applications will be discussed in later chapters.

The mnemonic technique known as the keyword method was experimentally employed as recently as 1975, by Richard Atkinson, to teach foreign language vocabulary. Students and instructors alike learned much more, and enjoyed learning more, when they used the keyword method. Michael Pressley first adapted the keyword method and applied it to school age populations, with equally impressive results. More recently, children from special education and remedial classes have been shown to make dramatic gains in learning when taught vocabulary using the keyword method.

USING THE KEYWORD METHOD

Purpose

An important purpose of the keyword method is to increase initial learning and delayed retention of unfamiliar vocabulary words. The method works by making unfamiliar vocabulary words more familiar, and by integrating those unfamiliar vocabulary words with the definition, strengthening both *encoding* (input) and *retrieval* (output) of information.

An Example

Let's try an example. A scientific word for typical members of the frog family is *ranid*. This word may be important to learn in order to understand some passages from a student's basal reader or science book. Ordinarily, teachers may attempt to teach such vocabulary words by having students say the words over and over to themselves, by showing them pictures of frogs and discussing the label *ranid*, by having students write the word many times in a notebook, or by making a flashcard, in which *ranid* is written on one side of a card, while *frog* is written on the other side, and practicing this word with other new vocabulary words. These activities are all based upon *rehearsal* — the notion that students who repeat this information often enough will remember it. In many cases, this is true. However, some students can practice or rehearse the information many times, and still forget the meaning of the word the following day. This happens because no meaningful *retrieval link* has been established between the stimulus (ranid) and the response (frog). If repetition alone does not bring forth the meaning of *ranid*, the student has no other means of retrieval.

The keyword method provides an explicit retrieval link, and reconstructs the unfamiliar word *ranid* to a more familiar, more easily remembered term. This process involves *reconstructing, relating,* and *retrieving,* the "three Rs" of the keyword method. Here is how it is done:

Reconstructing. Using the keyword method, teachers first reconstruct the unfamiliar vocabulary word to a similar-sounding *keyword* which is both concrete and familiar to the learner. A good keyword for *ranid* could be "rain," because: (1) rain sounds like ranid, (2) rain is familiar to students, and (3) rain is concrete enough to be easily pictured. Practice the new keyword with students until they can answer automatically. This shouldn't take much time because of the sound similarity between rain and ranid.

Relating. Once the keyword has been reconstructed and learned, it must be *related,* or linked, to the response, or to-be-learned information. In other words, using the *ranid* example, the keyword "rain" must be linked to the response, *frog.* This is done by combining *rain* and *frog,* in a sentence, visual image, or, best of all, in a picture which you can show to students. It is important that the keyword be doing something with, or interacting with, the to-be-remembered definition. A good interactive picture for **ranid** would be a picture of a *frog sitting in the rain.*

Notice that in this example the frog and the rain are linked together. This relating step is very important. Also notice that only the critical information to be learned is included in the picture. It is

Figure 2.1 Ranid (rain) = Frog

important to leave out anything in the picture (trees, birds, etc.) that is not necessary for remembering the information and might serve to create confusion.

Retrieving. After you have reconstructed the vocabulary word into a keyword and related it in a picture with its definition, you can teach students how to retrieve the definition. This step is fairly simple.

1. Tell students to think of the keyword when they are asked the definition of the vocabulary word. In the present example, for instance, when asked the meaning of *ranid*, students should first think of the keyword *rain*.

2. Tell students to think back to the interactive picture that contained the keyword and its definition. For example, once "rain" has been retrieved, it is easy to retrieve the picture of the *frog sitting in the rain.*

3. Finally, Tell students to retrieve the definition from the information in the picture. In the *ranid* example, it is easy to see that the definition is *frog*.

When you first present this method to your students, some students may respond with the keyword rather than the definition. For example, if you ask a student what *ranid* means, he or she may at first reply, "rain." If this happens, correct them by saying: "No, rain is only the keyword to help us remember the definition of ranid. What else was happening in the picture with the rain in it? Right, a *frog* was sitting in the rain. Therefore, ranid means *frog.*" Usually students do not have much difficulty with this step, but it is good to provide them with a little practice initially in learning that the keyword is not the definition, but merely a way to assist them in retrieving the definition, the appropriate response.

REVIEW: The three steps for the keyword method are:

1.   *Reconstruct* the term to-be-learned into an acoustically similar, already familiar, and easily pictured concrete term —select a keyword.

2.   *Relate* the keyword to the to-be-learned information in an interactive picture, image or sentence. (Remember, a picture will probably work best.)

3.   *Retrieve* the appropriate response: when asked what the response is: first, think of the keyword. Second, think back to the interactive picture and what was happening in that picture. Finally, state the desired response.

Additional examples. Here are some more examples for teaching vocabulary with the keyword method. The teacher wording below is meant only as a model. You may need to provide additional practice and review time for your own students, or conversely, you may wish to delete some of the teacher instructions. Later in this book, procedures are described for having students attempt to generate these pictures and images totally independently. (See Chapter 8)

Sample dialogue: "Students, today we are going to learn some new vocabulary words. I am going to teach you a brand new way of learning these words. I think you will like using this method of studying, and I want you to pay close attention.

"The first new word we are going to learn is *derelict. Derelict* is another word for a tramp. We all know what a tramp is, right? Now, I am going to teach you a keyword for *derelict.* A keyword is a word you already know, that sounds like the new word. It will help you remember the meaning of *derelict.* A good keyword for *derelict* is dairy, because *derelict* sounds like dairy, and we all know what a dairy cow is. When I ask you the keyword for *derelict* you should say dairy. What is the keyword for *derelict?* Good.

"Since you have learned the keyword for *derelict* is *dairy,* I am going to show you a picture with a dairy cow in it doing something with a tramp.

"See this picture of a tramp milking a dairy cow? What is happening in the picture? Good.

"Now I am going to show you how you can remember the new

word's definition. When I ask you what *derelict* means, first, you must think of the keyword. In this case our keyword is? ..... Right, dairy. Remember it is a word you already know, that sounds like *derelict*. Next, you need to think back to the picture that had the dairy in it and think about what was happening in that picture. What was happening in our picture with the dairy in it? Right, a *tramp was milking a dairy cow*. So then, what is the definition of derelict? Right, a tramp.

"Let's learn another word. *Dorado* is a kind of *fish*. A good keyword for *dorado* would be *door*, because it sounds like *dorado*, and you already know what it means. Now, look at this picture of a fish knocking at a door. What is happening in the picture? Right, a fish is knocking at a door. Now, if I ask you what dorado means, what do you think of first? Right, the keyword is door. Then you need to do what? Right, think back to the picture of the door and think of what was happening in that picture. What was happening in the picture with the fish? Right, the fish was knocking at a door. Finally, you are able to recall the new definition for *dorado*, or fish. Did anyone think that *dorado* means door? No, door is just the keyword to help us remember that dorado means fish."

You may find that some students perform better when they receive a little practice learning the keywords before being introduced to the picture. For example, you might introduce the vocabulary words and corresponding keywords prior to introducing the definitions. Below are some examples of vocabulary words and keywords. These words were used by Mastropieri, Scruggs, Levin, and Gaffney (1985), and Taylor (1982).

Vocabulary Word	*Keyword*
duct	duck
dahlia	doll
marmalade	mama
dogbane	dog
peavy	pea
garb	garbage
desperado	desk
barrister	bear
grotto	auto
sopor	soap

As you can see from the words and keywords in this list, the keywords are so similar in sound to the new vocabulary word that only a small amount of practice would be necessary to be able to master the list. Teachers can read each word and keyword for students and then have students say the keyword after hearing the vocabulary word. Typically, students can retrieve the corresponding

Interactive exercise

keyword after reviewing the list only once or twice.

The next step would be to introduce the interactive pictures, sentences, or images as in the listing below:

Word	Keyword	Definition	Interactive Sentence
Duct	(duck)	pipe	A duck standing inside a pipe.
Dahlia	(doll)	flower	A doll sniffing a flower.
marmalade	(mama)	jam	A mama spreading jam on toast.
dogbane	(dog)	tropical plant	A dog eating a tropical plant.
peavy	(pea)	hook	A pea stuck on the end of a hook.
garb	(garbage)	clothing	Garbage spilling over new clothing.
desperado	(desk)	outlaw	An outlaw holding up someone at a desk.
barrister	(bear)	lawyer	A bear pleading a case.
grotto	(auto)	cave	An auto driving into a cave.
sopor	(soap)	sleeping	A bar of soap sleeping.

Note that the keywords and their definitions are interacting in each of the examples. You can use these sentences to describe the interaction, and then ask your students to visualize and repeat the sentence to you. Or, better still, you could show actual line drawings of the pictures. Students also can draw their own pictures. It is important that you give students enough time to think about what is happening in each picture. After this, ask your students to practice retrieving the correct responses. You and your students will probably be surprised at how fast they can learn and remember new information!

You should also have your students practice retrieving the information backwards — that is, providing the new vocabulary word when asked the definition ("What was the new word we learned for *frog*?"). In this way, your students will be better able to respond with either the definition or the new word, depending on how the question is asked. This type of practice should help the new information become more readily accessible.

When students are initially learning the new definitions they rely heavily on the use of the keyword during the retrieval steps. However, after students have become more fluent with the new

words, and retrieval of the new definition is more automatic, they
will find they use the keywords less and less. In order to help develop
fluent responding, have the students practice on a worksheet of the
type shown below:

Interactive exercise

WORKSHEET
Directions: Fill in the blanks with the correct answers.

Word	Keyword	Definition	Interactive Sentence
Duct	(_____)	pipe	_____
Dahlia	(doll)	_____	A doll sniffing a _____.
_____	(mama)	jam	A mama spreading jam on toast.
dogbane	(_____)	tropical plant	_____ a tropical plant.
peavy	(_____)	hook	A _____ on the end of a hook.
_____	(garbage)	_____	Garbage spilling over new _____.
desperado	(____)	outlaw	An outlaw holding up someone at a ___.
barrister	(____)	lawyer	A _____ pleading a case.
grotto	(____)	cave	_____ into a cave.
_____	(soap)	sleeping	A bar of soap sleeping.

You should also provide opportunities for students to use the new
words in a variety of contexts, such as conversations and writing.
Practice in these contexts will help the new vocabulary to become
part of the students' working vocabulary, rather than simply the new
words for the week that are forgotten after the weekly test.

   Two types of practice activities have been especially helpful in
firming up responses. The first type requires students to *identify* the
correct information, while the second type requires students to
produce the new information. Identification formats are typically
easier than production formats. So provide activities that contain
identification formats first. For example, you could design worksheet activities for students to complete individually or in small
groups similar to the one below:

Identification Format

Directions: Select the appropriate word from list A and write it in the correct sentence.

List A: DUCT DAHLIA MARMALADE DOGBANE PEAVY GARB DESPERADO BARRISTER GROTTO SOPOR

1. A (*duct*) is another word meaning pipe.
2. Clothing is sometimes referred to as (*garb*).
3. The (*desperado*) ran from the police.
4. He put (*marmalade*) and peanut butter on his bread.
5. The (*barrister*) stood in front of the jury while she made her closing statements.
6. He was afraid to enter the dark (*grotto*) without a flashlight.
7. The (*dahlia*) had the biggest blossom in the whole bunch.
8. He used the (*peavy*) to hold and turn the log.
9. In the jungle the explorers chopped their way through the (*dogbane*).
10. The boring lecture brought on (*sopor*) for the tired student.

Production Format

Once your students have become fluent at identifying the new words in context, they are ready to produce them in both verbal and written formats. If the new vocabulary is not frequently used in class discussion and in readings, students may be less likely to have those words become part of their "working vocabularies". Activities similar to the ones below have been used with some success:

Production Format One

Write synonyms for each of the following words:
DUCT   DAHLIA   MARMALADE   DOGBANE   PEAVY GARB   DESPERADO   BARRISTER   GROTTO   SOPOR

Production Format Two

Use each of the new vocabulary words in a sentence. Or, write two paragraphs that contain each of this week's vocabulary words.

During these stages of instruction you should reinforce your students' accurate use of the new words in a variety of contexts. Try to point out times during conversations when the new words could be used, and perhaps structure specific times throughout the day for students to have opportunities to use the new vocabulary.

ABSTRACT VOCABULARY

So far, our examples have only applied to learning new labels for phenomena or concepts that students already know. Additionally, the examples supplied so far have consisted of fairly *concrete* vocabulary words. It is also very possible for the keyword method to be applied to *abstract vocabulary* learning, or the learning of labels for concepts that may not already be completely familiar. This section describes examples of how you can teach abstract vocabulary concepts with the keyword method.

Abstract vocabulary differs from concrete vocabulary in several ways. First, abstract vocabulary is much more difficult to visualize. Second, abstract vocabulary may represent instances of abstract concepts. And finally, abstract vocabulary may require longer, more complex definitions, rather than simple synonyms, as in the examples used previously.

The keyword method also works very well for teaching abstract vocabulary. You employ the same steps, *reconstructing*, *relating*, and *retrieving*, as described, to adapt abstract vocabulary to more meaningful, concrete, and memorable formats.

1. Identify one instance of the new abstract word for your own students, and then attempt to make that instance as concrete as possible.

2. Show that concrete instance interacting with the keyword in a picture, sentence, or image with the keyword.

An example. Consider the abstract word "surplus". Surplus is an abstract word that commonly means "having more than enough" of something.

1. *Reconstruct* "surplus" by creating a keyword for it. A good keyword for surplus would be "syrup" since it is familiar, easily pictured, and sounds like surplus.

2. In the *relating* step, show (or have your students imagine) a picture containing "lots of syrup bottles in the cupboards while someone is pouring way too much syrup over waffles."

3. Provide the *retrieving* step by telling students, when asked what "surplus" means, to think back to the keyword "syrup", remember there was *too much* syrup in the picture with the syrup in it, and finally remember that "surplus" means "having more than enough" of something. In this example the abstract concept

"surplus" has been made more concrete by showing one specific instance of the concept. You will need to make certain your students know that this is simply one example of surplus, that surplus can mean having more than enough of many different items, not merely syrup. However, once they have mastered the concept with the syrup example, they should have little difficulty with other examples. You should provide your students with many examples, after they have mastered the initial ones.

Several researchers, including Mastropieri, Scruggs and Fulk (1990) and Yuen (1985) adapted abstract vocabulary words using the keyword method. The examples listed below are some examples used by Yuen and include the abstract vocabulary words, the keywords, and the definitions. As you read the listing, try to generate an interactive sentence, illustration, or image that contains each keyword and appropriate definition. Remember that the keyword and definition should be doing something together.

	Word	*Keyword*	*Definition*
1.	celebrate	celery	having a party for something special
2.	intend	tent	when you mean to do something
3.	gesture	jacket	when you move your hand to show a feeling
4.	glisten	kitten	when something shines
5.	harvest	heart	when you gather crops like corn
6.	recite	the bike	when you repeat something from memory

How did you do? Below are some possible examples of interactive sentences. Compare your sentences with these examples. Then, make sure that your keyword and definition are really interacting.

Answers: Interactive Sentences

1. Celebrate (celery): Everyone at a special party is eating celery.
2. Intend (tent): Campers are standing around trying to put together tents.
3. Gesture (jacket): A person is pointing over at the row of jackets.
4. Glisten (kitten): A kitten that is shining very brightly.
5. Harvest (heart): People picking hearts off the plants (as in

picking heart-shaped tomatoes).

6.   Recite (the bike): Two bike riders are reciting poems or speeches.

You probably came up with sentences or images that were not exactly like the ones listed here. That is fine, as long as they meet the criteria of "interacting" or having the keyword doing something with the definition. It also may be helpful to include some explanatory dialogue to increase comprehension of the concept. For example, in the "intend" picture, one person may be depicted as saying, "I *intend* to set up a *tent*."

These mnemonic techniques improve initial learning as well as delayed recall of such abstract vocabulary. Students are also better able to comprehend and apply these words in a variety of contexts after being instructed mnemonically. Although you may wonder whether learning mnemonically might inhibit students' ability to use the words in other contexts, research has demonstrated the opposite: students are very good at applying information learned using such mnemonic techniques.

Below are more complex abstract vocabulary words listed only with their respective definitions. Spaces are provided for you to try to *first reconstruct* the word into a keyword. *Second, relate* the keyword to its respective definition. Develop an interactive sentence or picture. When you finish, write on a sheet of paper the correct definition without looking back (retrieve).

Vocabulary Word	Keyword	Definition	Interaction
vituperation		speaking abusively to someone	
objurgation		vehement chiding	
nonage		under the legal age	
saprophytic		living on decaying matter	
nepenthe		drug to decrease feelings of sorrow	
octroi		tax to pay on certain good entering a town	
amerce		to punish by imposing a fine	
bewray		to betray	
buncombe		empty or boring speech	
intercalate		to add days or weeks to the calendar	

How did you do? Check your keywords and interactive sentences with those we developed which are listed in the Appendix.

As you review our keywords and interactive sentences, remember that there is really no "one correct" response. There may be

Figure 2.2 Buncombe (bun) = Empty, Insincere Speech

Figure 2.3 Octroi (octopus) = Tax on Goods Entering A Town

several "good" keywords, and several "good" concrete instances of the definitions. To judge how effective your own mnemonic strategies are, ask yourself:

1. Can you easily retrieve the keyword upon hearing the main vocabulary word?

2. Does your keyword interact with the definition?

3. Are you able to easily retrieve the correct response?

Remember that certain words may be more familiar to you than they are to your students.

The most important consideration in creating keywords is the *level of familiarity* for your own students. Keep as a rule of thumb, keywords must be already familiar and sufficiently concrete for your own students, or they will not be successful.

WORD PARTS

Some scientific words are so complex they may require several keywords. Many times understanding the individual word parts is helpful for understanding the whole, larger word. Once students have learned the word parts, they are more likely able to determine the meaning of the complex words though they had never been taught them. Here are some examples you can try. Construct keywords and interactive pictures for these scientific word parts on your own!:

Word Part	Definition
bronto	thunder
paleo	old
sauro	lizard
thero	wild animal
ornith	bird
ptero	winged
poda	foot

(from Veit, Scruggs, & Mastropieri, 1986)

Remember the three steps: *reconstructing*, *relating*, and *retrieving*. Below are listed keywords and interactive sentences. See how they compare with the ones you developed independently. Remember, there may be several examples for each one that meet the necessary criteria. When you have finished, check your answers with ours in the Appendix.

Now, see if you can figure out the meanings of the following combinations of the word parts: (cover the extreme right column)

1. Pterosaurous: _____ (winged lizard)

2. Brontosaurus: _____ (thunder lizard)

3. Ornithopoda: _____ (bird footed)

4. Paleopoda: _____ (old foot)

5. Therapoda: _____ (wild animal footed)

Additional examples to practice this technique are provided in the science content area chapter.

FOREIGN LANGUAGE VOCABULARY

The first experimental applications of the keyword method involved learning foreign languages. In learning a foreign language, the new vocabulary is usually totally unfamiliar to the learner. Consequently, the keyword method is ideally suited for initial learning of new foreign language vocabulary. Mnemonic techniques have been used successfully to teach students Spanish and Italian vocabulary words (e.g., McLoone, Scruggs, Mastropieri, & Zucker, 1986; Scruggs, Mastropieri, Jorgensen, & Monson, 1986).

In the next table are some examples of Italian words and their English meanings. By this point, you should be getting familiar with how the method is applied. Remember the three steps: *reconstructing*, *relating*, and *retrieving*. Try to learn the following list of Italian vocabulary words using the keyword technique:

Italian Word	English Equivalent	Keyword	Interactive Sentence
1. roccia	cliff		
2. mela	apple		
3. coniglio	rabbit		
4. coltre	blanket		
5. capre	goat		
6. lago	lake		
7. carta	paper		
8. barca	boat		

9. fonda   bag
10. strada   road

Now compare your keywords and interactive images with the ones listed in the Appendix.

How did you do? By this point, you are probably well on your way to effectively using the mnemonic keyword method. The final sections of this chapter present additional applications for vocabulary learning and a sample mnemonic vocabulary lesson, while the remainder of the book presents additional applications for mnemonic learning in a variety of other content domains.

APPLICATIONS OF VOCABULARY LEARNING

This chapter has described steps to increase the initial acquisition and recall of new vocabulary. However, you will still need to have students practice using the new vocabulary in a variety of contexts if you intend to develop fluency with the new vocabulary and to have it become a part of your students' working vocabulary.

Once the information has been acquired initially, practice and use of the newly acquired information must be undertaken. It is usually recommended that lots of opportunities to use the new information are provided for students. These opportunities can be completed individually, in small groups, or in large groups. What is most critical is that everyone be able to have the necessary number of opportunities for practicing so the new vocabulary becomes very familiar and part of the working vocabulary. As mentioned earlier, these activities can require students to identify the new words as well as produce the new words. And, perhaps more importantly, this practice should take place in reading, writing, and speaking activities.

Identification Practice Activities Identification activities are easier tasks than production activities. You may first wish to develop activities for students to practice identifying the newly acquired vocabulary words. Identification formats present the new information and require students to select the appropriate response from a number of options, as in a multiple choice format or in a matching format. Let's see how well you learned some of the vocabulary presented in this chapter.

Directions: Read all the choices and then select the correct response for each item.

(a) Buncombe   (b) Amerce (c) Bewray   (d) Vituperation

(e) Saprophytic (f) Octroi   (g) Nonage   (h) Intercalate

(i) Nepenthe   (j) Objurgation

1.   speaking abusively to someone

2.   a vehement chiding

3.   legally underage for some activities

4.   living on decaying matter

5.   a drug to decrease feelings of sorrow

6.   a tax on certain goods entering a town

7.   to punish by imposing a fine

8.   to betray

9.   a boring speech

10. adding extra days to the calendar

(Answers: 1-d, 2-j, 3-g, 4-e, 5-i, 6-f, 7-b, 8-c, 9-a, 10-h)

Sample Production Practice Activity. A sample production practice activity modeled after the one just presented as an identification activity might consist of directions that required you to write the definitions of each of the words above (without, of course, seeing any of the stem alternatives). Let's see how well you mastered the Italian words you practiced earlier this chapter:

Italian Vocabulary Words Production Activity
Directions: Write the English definitions of each of the following words:

1.   roccia

2.   mela

3.   coniglio

4.   coltre

5.   capre

6.   lago

7.   carta

8.   barca

9.   fonda

10. strada

(answers: 1-cliff, 2-apple, 3-rabbit, 4-blanket, 5-goat, 6-lake, 7-paper, 8-boat, 9-bag, 10-road)

A MNEMONIC VOCABULARY LESSON

Following is an example of a classroom lesson using the keyword method to teach vocabulary. Although mnemonic techniques are used in this lesson, we have recommended in our book, *Effective Instruction for Special Education*, that important teacher effectiveness variables be included in *all* lessons, mnemonic or otherwise. Some overall components of critical importance in teaching a lesson are (1) review of previous information; (2) statement of lesson objective; (3) delivery of new information; (4) guided practice; (5) independent practice; and (6) formative, or ongoing, evaluation. Below is an abbreviated version of a mnemonic vocabulary lesson, with reference to these important lesson components. It should also be noted that this lesson is intended to represent dialogue that might take place in a class in which the students were already generally familiar with the techniques of mnemonic instruction.

Review Previous Information. Teacher: Last week we learned eight new vocabulary words. I will say the words one at a time, and we will see how many you remember [reviews words with class and provides feedback].

Statement of Lesson Objective. Today, I am going to introduce eight new vocabulary words that we will be learning about this week. I will give you the words, the keywords, and some pictures to help you learn the information. Later, we will practice remembering and using the words.

Presentation of New Information. Here are the new vocabulary words [shows overhead projection]. First, I will say the new words. Everyone say each word after I say it, when I signal:

Olfactory [signal]

Corridor [signal]

Canine [signal]

Cardiac [signal]

Loquacious [signal]

Affable [signal]

Hirsute [pronounced her-SOOT; signal]

Truculent [signal]

Let's try it one more time [repeats practice of list].

Now I'm going to give you the keywords for each of these words. Everybody repeat after me [writes on overhead as each keyword is introduced]:

The keyword for olfactory is *oil factory*. What is the keyword for olfactory? [Students respond, and teacher gives feedback as needed].

The keyword for corridor is *core*, like an apple core. What is the keyword for corridor?

The keyword for canine is *cane*. What is the keyword for canine?

The keyword for cardiac is *car*. What is the keyword for cardiac?

The keyword for loquacious is *lock*. What is the keyword for loquacious?

The keyword for affable is *laugh*. What is the keyword for affable?

The keyword for hirsute is *her suit*. What is the keyword for hirsute?

The keyword for truculent is *truck*. What is the keyword for truculent?

[Turns off overhead projector]. Now, when I say the new word, you tell me the keyword. [Goes over keywords again, calling on individual students and the class as a whole, and gives feedback as necessary].

So far we have learned the new words and the keywords which we will use to learn the meanings of the new words. Now I will show you the pictures. [Turns on overhead projector and shows mnemonic illustrations, in order]. Listen carefully and answer when I call on you:

Olfactory means *sense of smell*. The keyword for olfactory is *oil factory*. Remember this picture of people *smelling* an *oil factory*. Remember this picture of what? [calls on students] Right, people *smelling* an *oil factory*. And olfactory means what? [Calls on students].

Corridor means *hallway*. The keyword for corridor is *core*. Remember this picture of someone dropping an apple *core* in a *hallway*. Remember this picture of what? [Calls on students]. And corridor means what?

Canine means *dog*. The keyword for canine is *cane*. Remember this picture of a *dog* carrying a *cane*. Remember this picture of what? [Calls on students]. And canine means what? [Calls on students].

Cardiac means *heart*. The keyword for cardiac is *car*. Remember this picture of a *car* in the shape of a *heart*. Remember this picture of what? [Calls on students]. And cardiac means what? [Calls on students].

Loquacious means *talkative*. The keyword for loquacious is *lock*. Remember this picture of a *talkative lock*. Remember this picture of what? [Calls on students]. And loquacious means what? [Calls on students].

Affable means *agreeable* and *pleasant*. The keyword for affable is *laugh*. Remember this picture of a *pleasant, agreeable* person *laughing*. Remember this picture of what? [Calls on students]. And affable means what? [Calls on students].

Hirsute means *hairy* or *shaggy*. The keyword for hirsute is *her suit*. Remember this picture of a woman, and *her suit* is *hairy* and *shaggy*. Remember this picture of what? [Calls on students]. And hirsute means what? [Calls on students].

Truculent means *wild* and *fierce*. The keyword for truculent is *truck*. Remember this picture of a *wild* and *fierce* person driving a *truck*. Remember this picture of what? [Calls on students]. And truculent means what? [Calls on students].

Guided Practice

Now, let's go through the list without looking at the pictures. What does olfactory mean, Kim? Good, it means sense of smell. What was the keyword for olfactory, Gordon? Good, oil factory. Who can tell me the picture to remember the meaning of olfactory? OK, Bill. Good, people smelling an oil factory. [Repeat procedure for remaining words].

Now, let's try it the hard way. I'll give the meaning, and you tell me the new vocabulary word. OK, what word means heart, Ellen? Good, cardiac. And, what did you think of to help you remember that? Good, a car shaped like a heart. [Repeat procedure for remaining words].

Now, for the last thing we're going to do together for this lesson, I will give you a sentence, and you tell me how else you could say it. Who could say this sentence another way: The *cardiac* clinic was down the *corridor*. Jerry? Good, the heart clinic was down the hall. Now, who can say this sentence another way: The dog was smelly. Maria? Good, the canine bothered my olfactory sense. Rachael, would you rather have a *canine* that was *affable* or a *canine* that was *truculent*? Why would you rather have an affable canine? What does the sentence mean? Good, a pleasant and agreeable dog, or a wild and fierce dog. [Repeat procedure for remaining words].

Independent Practice

With the time left in the period, I am going to give you a worksheet, where you will answer some of these questions on your own. When you finish the first page, turn and do the second page, without looking at the first. If you have any questions, raise your hand [Hands out the following worksheets]:

WORKSHEET 1

Fill in the blanks:

New Word	Keyword	Definition	Picture
Olfactory	_____	_____	_____
_____	Core	_____	_____
_____	_____	_____	A talkative lock.
_____	_____	Dog	_____
_____	Her suit	_____	_____
Truculent	_____	_____	_____
_____	_____	pleasant,agreeable	_____
_____	_____	_____	A heart-shaped car.

WORKSHEET 2

Fill in the blanks:

Word	Keyword	Definition	Picture
Loquacious	_____	_____	_____
Affable	_____	_____	_____
Corridor	_____	_____	_____
Cardiac	_____	_____	_____
Truculent	_____	_____	_____
Canine	_____	_____	_____
Hirsute	_____	_____	_____
Olfactory	_____	_____	_____

Turn in when you have finished.

Evaluation. Now, everyone put everything away but a pencil and a piece of paper. I'll say the words one at a time and you write the meanings. [Gives evaluation measure].

SUMMARY

The lesson provided above is simply a sample of one which you might give to your students. Of course, you will have to adapt the instruction for the words your students need to learn, as well as the students' ages and ability levels.

This chapter has presented the basic rules for using the keyword method. Again they are:

1. *Reconstruct* the term to-be-learned into an acoustically similar, already familiar, and easily pictured concrete term (keyword).

2. *Relate* the keyword with the to-be-learned information in an interactive picture, image or sentence. (Remember, a picture will probably work best.)

3. Teach your students to *Retrieve* the appropriate response: when asked about a particular word, first, think of the keyword; next, think of the picture with the keyword in it, think of what *else* is happening in the picture, and retrieve the correct answer.

When implemented properly, the keyword method will help your students learn more vocabulary words in a shorter time period, and will help them recall those words over lengthy delay intervals. The basic premise of the method is to make unfamiliar information more familiar and more meaningful, and to integrate the definitions of the new words with the keyword.

The keyword method is a versatile technique, which can be used to teach information other than vocabulary words. Some following chapters will present how adaptations of this technique can be used to teach many types of information in addition to the vocabulary information just presented. You should attempt to work through all the practice activities that are presented in this volume. In this way, by the time you complete the text, you should have mastered many of the steps necessary for facilitating your learning and memory, and you will be better able to teach them to your students.

CHAPTER 3

Pegwords, Acronyms, Acrostics, and Phonetic Mnemonics

It is often important for students to learn and remember information which occurs in a series. In other words, sometimes students need to learn a connected *set* of responses, rather than a single response, to a given stimulus, or question. Such information includes the names of the Great Lakes, or the first ten amendments of the U.S. Constitution. It could include a sequence, in order, of steps in a procedure: writing a check, using a table saw, or getting lunch in a cafeteria. In some cases, the *order*, or sequence, of the information is important; in other cases, such as a list of items to be obtained from a grocery store or a library, order is less important.

A variety of mnemonic techniques can be used for teaching serial list information. In this chapter, each technique is described from simplest to the most complex application.

ACRONYMS AND ACROSTICS: THE "FIRST LETTER" STRATEGIES

Sometimes information is relatively familiar to learners, so that only a minimal prompt can activate recall. In such cases, "first letter" strategies can be helpful. The strategy often takes the form of an *acronym*, each letter in the acronym represents the first letter in a word on the response list. Since the first letter is only a minimal prompt, it is important that the set of responses be familiar enough to students for the strategy to be useful. It is also important to have the student link the acronym to the appropriate list.

Acronyms

The first example is one to most people who have studied geography in school. To teach the names of the Great Lakes, give students the acronym "HOMES." Each letter in the word HOMES stands for the first letter of one of the five Great Lakes: Huron, Ontario, Michigan, Erie, and Superior. This particular strategy has proved effective for several generations of school children. But it is important to be certain the individual names of the Great Lakes are familiar enough so that the first letter will serve as a sufficient prompt. If your students are unfamiliar with the name **Ontario**, you need to practice that name until you feel certain that the letter "O" can prompt "Ontario."

It is important that students have a means to retrieve HOMES when asked for the names of the Great Lakes. Students can learn the names of the lakes and learn the acronym for retrieving them, but forget to connect the acronym to the names of the Great Lakes. To strengthen this association, it may be helpful to picture (or ask your students to imagine) a scene of *homes* placid at the edge of *large lakes*. When thinking of the names of Great Lakes, then, students can remember the picture of lakes, remember that Homes were there, and then retrieve the individual names through use of the acronym.

Another example of a first letter strategy teaches the names of the four voices in a quartet. Think of someone about to *STAB* a quartet. The first letters of STAB stand for Soprano, Tenor, Alto, and Bass (from Lorayne and Lucas' *The Memory Book*) (1974).

In general, first letter strategies are most helpful when the items to be remembered are concrete and very familiar.

Lists of information often do not contain first letters which easily form themselves into words, or require so much manipulation that the purpose of enhancing memory may be lost. In some cases, clusters of letters which are in themselves easily remembered can replace acronyms. For example, principal industries of the state of Arizona can be retrieved by recalling the "4Cs": Cotton, Copper, Citrus, and Climate (i.e., tourism). Another common example uses an acronym, "ROY G. BIV", to recall the colors of the spectrum (Red, Orange, Yellow, Green, Blue, Indigo, and Violet). The advantage of this particular **acronym** is that it also presents colors in the order in which they appear in the spectrum of visible light. A disadvantage is that the name, **Roy G. Biv,** does not denote a real person and lacks familiarity. This disadvantage can be handled by having the students repeat the name, increasing familiarity. Or, additionally, an image of a **"Roy G. Biv"** dressed in all the colors of the rainbow could help retrieve the name, given the question, "Name all the colors of the spectrum."

Acrostics

Acrostics are the opposites of acronyms, in that a sentence is provided to retrieve letters. The first letter of each word in the sentence, then, represents a target, to-be-remembered letter. Many people are familiar with the acrostic, "Every good boy deserves fudge," to denote the notes on the lines of the treble clef. (The notes representing the spaces in the treble clef are often denoted by the acronym,

"FACE", where each letter stands for a note). Another use of the acrostic is in spelling difficult words, such as in the acrostic, *"George's elderly old grandfather rode a pig home yesterday,"* to promote recall of the spelling of the word, **"geography."** This method for teaching the spellings of more than a handful of target words may prove cumbersome, however. The reader is encouraged to examine Chapter 7 for further information on spelling mnemonics.

RHYMING MNEMONICS

Overall, first letter mnemonics represent some of the most familiar mnemonics used by students in school. Many adults can recall using these mnemonics to assist them in studying for tests. Often people report having developed these strategies independently.

Some of the strategies for promoting recall of numbered or ordered information which follow, however, may be less familiar to readers. One example which may serve as a transition is a rhyming strategy for remembering the English-language names of the constellations of the zodiac, in order. In this case, a first letter strategy may not be appropriate because it is difficult to construct a meaningful word out of these names, which would read, "R-B-T-C-L-V-S-S-A-G-W-F." However, by using parts of each of the words, a plausible rhyme can be constructed (offered by H.A. Rey in his book, *The Stars*): "The ramble twins crab liverish/ Scaly scorpions are good water-fish." In this case, words and syllables prompt recall of constellation names:

Ramble	=	ram, bull (Aries, Taurus)
Twins	=	twins (Gemini)
Crab	=	crab (Cancer)
Liverish	=	lion, virgin (Leo, Virgo)
Scaly	=	scales (Libra)
Scorpions	=	scorpion (Scorpio)
Are	=	Archer (Sagittarius)
Good	=	Goat (Capricorn)
Waterfish	=	Watercarrier, fish (Aquarius, Pisces)

THE PEGWORD

The pegword is a rhyming system for remembering numbers. These numbers are then related, through interactive pictures or images, to information associated with numbers. Pegwords are usually developed for numbers one through ten:

one = bun or gun or sun

two = shoe

three = tree

four = door or floor

five = hive

six = sticks

seven = heaven

eight = gate

nine = vine, line, or lion

ten = hen

William Browning, in his book *Memory Power for Exams,* includes pegwords for numbers 11-20:

eleven = lever

twelve = elf

thirteen = thirsting

fourteen = forking

fifteen = fixing

sixteen = sitting

seventeen = severing

eighteen = aiding

nineteen = knighting

twenty = twinty (twins)

An example. The simplest use of the pegword method is when remembering a list of familiar things. For example, suppose you are going to the store and need to remember to buy hot dogs, bananas, milk, soda, and fish. You could construct the following pegword system:

Number	Pegword	Item	Picture
1	Bun	Hot Dogs	Hot Dogs in a Bun
2	Shoe	Milk	Milk being poured into a Shoe
3	Tree	Bananas	Bananas in a Tree
4	Floor	Soda	Soda spilling on the Floor
5	Hive	Fish	Bees taking a Fish to a Hive

In this case, the order of the items is probably not important. However, the pegword system does provide a series of systematic prompts (bun, shoe, tree, etc.) that can ensure the entire list will be remembered.

Practice studying this list yourself. First, be sure that you can easily recite the pegwords. Then, one at a time, construct a picture or mental image of each grocery item on the list. The best method, especially if you are teaching this content, is to draw the picture, and recite the retrieval steps as you draw and examine the picture. It is not important that the picture be artistic; simply that the interaction is recognizable and that you study it.

It is also possible to construct a visual image. In this case, it is important that you actively construct the image, think about it, and examine it for detail. For example, it may be easy to think of the sentence, "Milk being poured into a shoe." But, if you have accurately and completely constructed the visual image, you should be able to answer questions such as: "What type of shoe is it?" "What type of container is the milk being poured from?" "What type of milk is it?" "How is the milk being poured?" If you can answer a number of questions like this, you can be sure you have formed an effective visual image.

For the final step, practice retrieving the five items to yourself, using the pegword system. First, think of the number. Then, think of the pegword. Then, think of the interactive picture or image you created. Finally, retrieve the answer and move to the next number. If you have practiced correctly, you will be surprised to note how effective this pegword system is.

At this point, you may be asking, "Why don't I simply *write down* the items in the grocery list, so that I don't have to memorize in the first place?" Of course you can. This type of memory is called *external memory*, and in many cases is the most effective means of remembering things (given, of course, that you remember to bring the list!). However, in many instances, particularly in school, it is not possible to write down information for later reference, such as on a test. Teachers should help students understand when "external memory" devices are helpful and when they are not.

Tolfa, Scruggs, and Mastropieri (1987) recently investigated the use of the pegword system to help students remember some possible causes of dinosaur extinction. For each of nine possible reasons, the list was developed as follows:

Number	Pegword	Reason	Interactive Picture
1	Bun	Climate became cold	Cold dinosaur holding frozen *buns*.
2	Shoe	Swamps dried up.	Dinosaur with *shoes* trying to enter dry swamp.

3	Tree	Exploding star.	Dinosaurs around a Christmas *Tree* watching the star on top explode.
4	Door	Small mammals ate eggs.	Small mammals breaking, destroying and eating dinosaur eggs on a *door*.
5	Hive	Disease	Sick dinosaur watching a *hive*.
6	Six	Too big and clumsy to survive.	Big, clumsy dinosaur tripping on *sticks*.
7	Heaven	Poisoned by newly emerging plants	Dinosaur eating poison, dying, and going to *heaven*.
8	Gate	Food sources disappeared.	Hungry-looking dinosaur looking at a *gate* on which a sign reads, "No food inside."
9	Vine	Killed each other off.	Dinosaurs fighting, while tangled in *vines*.

Figure 3.1 Possible Reason for Dinosaur Extinction #2 (shoe) = Swamps Dried Up

Learning disabled students who had studied these pictures were more than twice as likely to recall the information than learning disabled students who had spent the same amount of time studying more traditional, representational pictures. In this case, the possible reasons for dinosaur extinction were numbered in order of their plausibility as an explanation. However, as with the grocery list example, it is not necessary that items to be remembered follow any special order. The pegword system helps ensure that all information will be retrieved.

A list such as the one above could be very helpful in a variety of school tasks, such as in remembering reasons offered why Shakespeare may not have written all the plays attributed to him, the numbered causes of the Civil War, or a list of principal exports from a specific country.

In some cases, it may be helpful to develop mnemonic pegword pictures which include some element of the target stimulus within each, so that multiple lists will not be confused. For example, all the pegword pictures for dinosaur extinction included some picture or reference to dinosaurs. This can help ensure that these causes will not be confused with some other set of natural causes students may have to learn.

Figure 3.2 Possible Reason for Dinosaur Extinction #7 (heaven) = Plants Became Poisonous

USING KEYWORDS AND PEGWORDS

Sometimes, numbers are associated with unfamiliar names of things, and a combined keyword-pegword strategy facilitates mnemonic learning. One example is in learning hardness levels (according to Moh's scale) of minerals. The hardness scale indicates which minerals are harder than other minerals. For example, diamond, the hardest of the minerals, has a hardness level of 10, while talc, one of the softest minerals, has a hardness level of 1. Any mineral with a hardness level of, for example, four, is harder (i.e., can scratch) a mineral with a hardness level of three or lower.

Remembering the hardness levels of minerals can be very difficult for students because many mineral names are unfamiliar, and because numbers are difficult-to-remember abstractions. By combining a keyword for the mineral name with a pegword for the mineral hardness level in an interactive picture, a strong, memorable association can be developed. Some examples are given below:

Mineral	Keyword	Hardness	Pegword	Picture
Talc	Tail	1	Bun	Animal with a *bun* on its *tail*.
Crocoite	Crocodile	2	Shoe	A *crocodile* wearing *shoes*.
Antimony	Ant	3	Tree	*Ants* climbing up a tree.
Wolframite	Wolf	4	Door	A *wolf* looking in a *door*.
Hornblende	Horn	5	Hive	A *hive* in a *horn*.
Garnet	Garden	6	Sticks	A *garden* of *sticks*.
Quartz	Quarter	7	Heaven	A *quarter* in *heaven*.
Topaz	Top	8	Gate	A *top* spinning on a *gate*.
Corundum	Car	9	Vine	A *car* tangled in *vines*.
Diamond	Diamond	10	Hen	A *hen* wearing a *diamond*.

You will notice that the last mineral, **diamond**, did not have a keyword because **diamond** is already familiar to most students. A picture of a **diamond** will be easily recognizable. In such cases, a keyword is not necessary. This type of reconstruction is called a *mimetic* reconstruction, in which concrete, familiar words are drawn (or imagined) literally. More information on this technique is presented later.

Whenever teaching mnemonically, it is important to practice all the steps of the retrieval process, so that students can tell you not just the correct answer, but the steps they took to retrieve the correct

Figure 3.3 Garnet (garden) = Hardness Level Six (sticks)

answer. In many cases, information which is not effectively connected will soon be forgotten.

A Practice Example: Now, you try developing a pegword list for the hardness levels of the following minerals. When you have finished, practice and test yourself on the answers. Our keywords and pictures are provided in the appendix. Don't worry if you didn't arrive at the same keywords and pictures we offer. Many alternatives are possible. The most important things to remember in constructing pictures and images are to make sure

(1) that keywords sound very much like the information to be remembered,

(2) that the keywords are likely to be familiar to the learners, and

(3) that stimulus information is effectively related to response information in an interactive picture.

Here are the mineral names and associated hardness levels:

Name	Keyword	Hardness	Pegword	Picture
Bauxite		1	Bun	
Gypsum		2	Shoe	
Calcite		3	Tree	

Rhodochrosite	4	Door
Apatite	5	Hive
Feldspar	6	Sticks
Starolite	7	Heaven
Beryl	8	Gate

When you have developed images and practiced them, test yourself. Then turn to the appendix and compare your list of keywords and pictures with our list.

More Practice

Children in school are often asked to remember the planets of our solar system in their order from the sun. You can help students learn and remember this information by developing a pegword system. Here are the planets in order from the sun:

Planet	Keyword	Number	Pegword	Picture
Mercury		1	Bun	
Venus		2	Shoe	
Earth		3	Tree	
Mars		4	Door	
Jupiter		5	Hive	
Saturn		6	Sticks	
Uranus		7	Heaven	
Neptune		8	Gate	
Pluto		9	Vine	

First, think of a keyword for each of the planets. Then, picture each of the keywords interacting with their corresponding pegword and construct a picture. Practice retrieving the information, and test your recall. Then, turn to the appendix and compare your mnemonic strategies with the ones listed there.

PHONETIC MNEMONICS

Sometimes it is important to remember not just a single number or number series, but a long string of numbers. Such number strings could include telephone numbers, locker combinations, or dates in history. For these purposes, the pegword system may not be adequate. A mnemonic for transforming number series into words, known as phonetic mnemonics, was developed many years ago, and reported as early as 1890, in William James' *Principles of Psychology*. Using phonetic mnemonics, each number is reconstructed into a corresponding consonant sound. These consonant sounds and associated numbers are as follows:

Number	Sound
0	s or z
1	t or d
2	n
3	m
4	r
5	l
6	sh, ch (or tch), j, soft g
7	k, hard c, hard g
8	f
9	p or b

Vowels (which have no numerical meaning) are then inserted among the consonants to produce memorable words. For example, to remember the number 92, you can construct a word from the consonant sounds, p (or b) and n. The words *"pin," "bin,"* and *"bone"* would all be acceptable phonetic mnemonics for the number 92. The words "door pin," "tar bone," or "terrapin," ("rr" = one "r" sound) could be phonetic mnemonics for 1492. One difficulty with this mnemonic technique is that the number-letter associations are more difficult to remember than are, for example, the rhyming pegwords, and therefore more time is needed to learn them. One helpful way to get started learning the mnemonic system is to memorize the sentence, "Satan may relish coffee pie." The consonants in this sentence provide the order of the corresponding numbers:

Satan may relish coffee pie.
0 1 2 3   4 5 6 7 8   9

Another method, suggested by Lorayne and Lucas in *The Memory Book*, provides associative links for each number:

0   The first letter in zero is z.

1   T has one downstroke.

2   N has two downstrokes.

3   <u>M</u> has three downstrokes.

4   <u>R</u> is the last letter in the word four.

5   <u>L</u> is formed by the five fingers, thumb out.

6   <u>J</u> is nearly the mirror image of 6.

7   <u>K</u> can be formed by two 7s, back to back.

8   8 looks like handwritten <u>f</u>.

9   9 is the mirror image of <u>P</u>.

Using these number-letter associations, a word-picture can be produced for many number patterns that need to be remembered. For example, to remember a telephone number of a builder, 947-2711, the mnemonic phrase, **"Poor King Tut"** can be constructed and an image of a **Poor King Tut** *building* **his own pyramid.** To remember the address 2082, a phonetic mnemonic could be constructed of a "nose-phone," and an image of the person living at #2082 dialing a phone with his or her nose. To remember locker combination 25-36-42, the three phonetic words "nail," "match," "rain" could be constructed and a picture or image of someone driving a *nail* into a *match* in the *rain*. Remembering the sequence of these number-words, of course, is critical. For a final example, to remember the date 1453, the year of the fall of Constantinople, the words "deer-lame" could be constructed from the numbers. An image could then be constructed of a *deer* going *lame* in a scene associated with the fall of Constantinople. Lorayne and Lucas, in *The Memory Book*, list phonetic mnemonics for numbers 1-100.

Some caution should be exercised when attempting to use this mnemonic with children who have learning difficulties. It is perhaps the most complicated of the mnemonic systems in this book to execute. Care should be taken to ensure sufficient practice for easy retrieval of the numbers. Since the method is so complex, be sure that specific information might not be acquired more rapidly using simpler methods, such as rehearsal. Some additional mnemonic strategies for remembering digits are provided in the mathematics section.

For some students the phonetic mnemonic may prove to be very useful. Students may enjoy playing this game with each other.

A SAMPLE LESSON: A MNEMONIC MINERAL LESSON

Here is a possible lesson to help students remember hardness levels of specific minerals. The lesson is presented in abbreviated form:

Review of Previous Information. Teacher: We have been talking about minerals and their properties. Let's cover what we have learned so far. What is a mineral, Ramon? [Completes daily review].

Statement of Lesson Objective We have discussed the property of *hardness* of a mineral, and why it is important in knowing the usefulness and value of the mineral. Today we will learn the hardness levels of some North American minerals. To learn them, we will use the keyword and pegword methods we have practiced earlier. After that, you will work, and we will take a brief quiz to see how much you learned.

Presentation of New Information. [Show a list of mineral names on overhead projector]. Here are the minerals and keywords we will be learning about. Everyone say them after me:

Talc	Crocoite	Antimony	Wolframite	Hornblende
Garnet	Quartz	Topaz	Corundum	Diamond

[Shows overhead of minerals and keywords; see page 38]

Now let's practice the minerals and their keywords [Rehearses list, questions, and provides feedback].

You already know the pegword system, so let's go over the minerals and hardness levels:

Talc is number *one* on the hardness scale. The keyword for talc is *tail*. What is the keyword for talc? Good, tail. The pegword for number *one* is *bun*. What is the pegword for one? Good, bun. To remember that talc is one on the hardness scale, think of this picture of a *bun* on a *tail*. When I ask you for the hardness level of talc, remember the keyword, **tail**, think of the picture with the tail in it, remember the **tail had a bun on it**, and give me the answer, one. Now, what is the hardness level of talc? Good, one. How did you remember that? (Provide feedback on retrieval steps).[Repeat for remaining nine minerals].

Guided Practice. Now, let's try it the hard way. I will give you a mineral hardness number and you tell me the mineral name. Who can tell me the mineral with the hardness level of seven? Joey? Good, quartz. How did you remember that? Good, the picture of the **quarter in heaven**. [Repeat for remaining minerals].

Independent Practice. Now I'd like you to complete this worksheet. Ask me if you have any questions. [Hands out worksheet]:

Mineral	Keyword	Hardness	Pegword	Picture
Talc	_____	___	Bun	Animal with a ____ on its _____.
_____	Crocodile	2	____	A _____ wearing _____.
Antimony	_____	___	_____	_____ climbing up a tree.

	Wolf	4		A *wolf* looking in a _____.
Hornblende	____	__	Hive	A *hive* in a _____.
	Garden	6	____	A *garden* of _____.
Quartz	_____	7	____	A _____ in _____.
	Top	__	Gate	A *top* spinning on a *gate*.
Corundum	____	9	____	A ___ tangled in _____.
Diamond	_____	10	____	A ___ wearing a _____.

Evaluation. Now, everybody take out a piece of paper and pencil. When I say the name of a mineral, you write down the number. Then, when I say a hardness number, you write the mineral name.

SUMMARY

This chapter described the use of pegwords, acrostics, acronyms, and phonetic mnemonics for learning lists of information or information that occurs in a series. List learning strategies, of the type described in this chapter, can be applied to any type of list information that your students need to recall. These strategies are often best employed in conjunction with other strategies for learning related information, such as those described in the next chapter.

CHAPTER 4

Reconstructive Elaborations: An Integrative Model

This chapter describes the model of **reconstructive elaborations** we use to adapt all content area information so it can be taught using mnemonic techniques. The model incorporates many elements of what we have described in the earlier chapters but expands on them. This model takes account of the meaningfulness and familiarity of the material and its concreteness.

When we organized the instruction of special education students to make use of reconstructive elaborations, we found that students taught using this system learned over twice as much content and retained it over long periods of time. Teachers who used our materials reported their students appeared more motivated to learn in class and participated more in class discussions. Students not only increased their test grades, but also increased their report card grades from D's and F's to A's & B's. The students reported they would like their teachers to use similar materials in almost every other subject. They attributed their performance gains to the use of the mnemonic strategies.

Teachers requested that we provide them with mnemonic materials for every subject they taught. We could not do this for them, but, after reading this chapter, you can develop these materials for your students to use.

The model of *reconstructive elaborations* uses elements from the earlier chapters describing the keyword and pegword techniques. In this chapter we first provide a definition and then examples of how the reconstructive elaborations model can be applied to geography, history, and other social studies material.

THE RECONSTRUCTIVE ELABORATIONS MODEL

Reconstructive elaborations makes unfamiliar content more **familiar**, nonmeaningful information more **meaningful**, and abstract information more **concrete**. Information to be remembered are elaborated (**linked** together) so they will be better remembered.

Definition of the Reconstructive Component

The **reconstructive** component helps adapt the content to more familiar and more meaningful formats. Social studies content ranges from very meaningful and very familiar to unfamiliar and nonmeaningful. The degree to which novel content is familiar and meaningful depends upon the prior knowledge of the students. When you use these techniques, keep in mind the background knowledge of the particular students you are teaching.

We have developed three types of reconstructions depending upon the level of meaningfulness and familiarity: mi**metic**, **symbolic**, and **acoustic** reconstructions. All three types are meant to represent information in pictorial formats to assist in making the novel content more concrete, more familiar, and more meaningful. Each type of reconstruction is described separately below.

Mimetic reconstructions. Mimetic reconstructions are simply pictorial representations of the actual information to be learned. Any content that is already meaningful and familiar to the students can be made more concrete by depicting it in an actual illustration or image. For example, many social studies textbooks introduce content that is meaningful and familiar to students with such notions as *early bridges* or *trenches*. We recommend that teachers reconstruct this information mimetically, for instance, presenting students with actual illustrations of early bridges or trenches, so the concepts of what is meant by *early bridges* or *trenches* can be clearly understood from the beginning.

When content in geography or history is presented that is already familiar and meaningful, a mimetic reconstruction or an *actual picture* of the information will assist in making that content more concrete for the students. **But one must know what is familiar to the students.** For example, if they are familiar with President Kennedy, then a simple mimetic reconstruction, or picture, would be sufficient. But if they don't know who he was, such a picture (mimetic reconstruction) would not be useful.

We have misjudged our students' prior knowledge. During the fall of 1988, the U.S. had convoys protecting the oil ships in the Persian Gulf. Since information regarding these convoys was in the newspapers daily and on television, we assumed our learning disabled high school students would be familiar with the word *convoy*. Therefore, we showed them a picture of a convoy, assumed they knew what it was, and used it in our teaching. To our chagrin, we learned that none of the students knew what the word *convoy* meant. Our mimetic reconstruction was of little assistance.

Mimetic reconstructions can be in the **stimulus** (question) or in the **response** (answer) portion. In other words, if the question was: "What were early bridges like?", the mimetic picture of a bridge would be the stimulus portion of the item. However, if the early bridges item—"were no good and often rotted and washed away"— were reversed and the question became: "What often rotted and washed away?", the early bridge mimetic reconstruction would become the response component. The elaboration component section provides additional examples of how to use reconstructions as part of the question (stimulus) or part of the answer (response).

Symbolic reconstructions. Symbolic reconstructions represent abstract pieces of information, intended to make the information more concrete and therefore more meaningful for students. Many terms in social studies are initially abstract. For example, in discussing information on people and their cultures, various religions, or economic practices, the terminology will be initially strange and unfamiliar to students. Teachers can symbolize these concepts by selecting familiar pictures or symbols that are already meaningful to students. But one might introduce topics in religion by picturing a church. Culture might be made more concrete through a symbolic pictures of people from different tribes dressed in native garb, while an economic policy might be symbolized pictorially as people receiving services in a hospital clinic or homeless people receiving food at a public kitchen. Other concepts involved in government and economics would need to be symbolized in pictures to help the students understand the underlying concepts.

Political cartoonists use this type of reconstruction in their

Figure 4.1 Early Bridges Often Rotted and Washed Away

editorial cartoons. Around election times, the drawings of the elephant for the Republican Party or the mule for the Democratic Party are used widely in advertising and on the news media. These are also examples of symbolic reconstructions of information, in that the elephant symbolizes the Republican Party, and the mule symbolizes the Democratic Party. These two examples work very well with most educated Americans.

We found, however, that many special education students in junior high schools did not know that an elephant represented one party and a mule the other. In this case, these examples are not good *symbolic reconstructions*, because the symbolized information is unfamiliar and nonmeaningful to the particular students.

As in the mimetic reconstructions, symbolic reconstructions can be in either the **stimulus** component (question) or the **response** component (answer). The main criterion to use in developing such symbolic reconstructions is that they consist of something that is already familiar and meaningful to students.

Acoustic reconstructions. Sometimes information is totally unfamiliar to students. When this is the case, the only thing familiar about the new information is that it *sounds like something else that is familiar.* When information is totally unfamiliar, that information can be reconstructed *acoustically* into something familiar by using the steps described in the keyword method chapter (Chapter 2).

For example, many unfamiliar names of famous people are introduced throughout social studies. These names can be reconstructed acoustically using the same steps that were used to reconstruct keywords for learning new vocabulary. Remember how the Italian word *roccia* was turned into a keyword that consisted of something acoustically similar, already familiar, and easily pictured: *roach.* The same steps can be used in reconstructing unfamiliar names of people, places, or things.

To learn, for example, that George M. Cohan was a famous American songwriter during World War I who wrote the song, "Over There," a keyword can be constructed for *Cohan.* In this case, *cone* (as in ice cream cone) would be a good acoustic reconstruction for Cohan because it *sounds like* Cohan, and is already familiar and meaningful to students.

The next step is to construct an interactive picture, image or sentence of an ice cream cone and the to-be-remembered information doing something together. In this case the to-be-remembered information consists of the fact that George M. Cohan composed the song entitled "Over There." A good interactive image is shown below: Children eating ice cream cones and being asked by someone, "Where did you get those cones?" The children, while pointing to an ice cream stand, respond in singsong voices by saying: "Over there, over there."

Notice that this example meets all the criteria for developing an effective keyword strategy for learning unfamiliar vocabulary words, but this time the steps have been applied to learning an accomplishment of a famous person.

These identical procedures can be applied to learning the names of unfamiliar places and what they are noted for. For example, the Battle of Bunker Hill took place during the American Revolutionary War and is considered an important battle. At the Battle of Bunker Hill the British were victorious in defeating the Continental Army, but they also suffered severe losses. The name of Bunker Hill is probably unfamiliar to most beginning history students, and so the associated information—that the British defeated the American Continental Army, but also suffered many losses—will be difficult to remember.

An acoustic reconstruction can be made of Bunker Hill. *Bumper* sounds like bunker, is familiar to students, and is easily pictured. If the Battle of Bunker (Bumper) Hill is encoded to include an interactive scene of a hill covered with bumpers, (for Bunker), with the "red coats" (for British) defeating the American Continental Army, while also showing the British suffering many losses, then recall and later retrieval will be easier.

The information could be retrieved similarly to the keyword method. First when asked about Bunker Hill, think of the keyword: *Bumper Hill*. Second, think back to the picture that contained the bumpers and think about what was happening in that picture. Third,

Figure 4.2 George M. Cohan (cone) = Composed the Song "Over There"

retrieve the appropriate information: that the Battle of Bunker Hill was fought during the Revolutionary War, the British defeated the American Continental Army, but they suffered many losses.

Summary Information on the Reconstructive Component

The reconstructive component is the first step undertaken to make the information more familiar, meaningful, and concrete. Novel information can be reconstructed three ways. Mimetic reconstructions simply represent the information in pictorial formats because that information is assumed to be already familiar and meaningful for students. **Symbolic reconstructions** convey abstract information but it is made pictorially familiar for students. **Acoustic reconstructions** reconstruct totally unfamiliar information into acoustically similar, already familiar, and easily pictured information and depict it interacting with the to-be-remembered response. The principles for acoustic reconstructions are identical to those used in the keyword method: reconstructing, relating, and retrieving.

The Elaboration Component

The elaboration component is the **linking component** of the model. This component is extremely critical and must be included if the new

Figure 4.3 Battle of Bunker Hill (Bumper Hill) = British Won, with Heavy Losses

content is to be remembered accurately. A good elaboration provides a link between the two or more pieces of information that are to be recalled together. Unfortunately, most textbooks and teachers do not provide effective **elaborations** or **links** to assist students with what they consider the important information to remember.

For example, in the early bridges example presented earlier, the social studies textbook simply states that early bridges were made of wood laid across streams and they often rotted and washed away, and therefore were not good. A good reconstructive elaboration would present mimetic pictures of each of those two components: *early bridges* and *what they were made of* and show them decayed, in bad repair, rotting away. We have used a picture of an early pioneer standing at the edge of a stream looking at an early bridge made of logs in which part of it is rotting and washing away. The early pioneer is saying: "Dang, these early bridges are no good!" Notice that the two pieces of information are interacting or doing something together, as in the keyword and pegword examples presented earlier.

The elaboration component creates a direct connection between the question and its response. This type of interaction of the pieces of information facilitates recall of the content to be remembered. We have found that even primary-age mentally retarded children's learning can be facilitated with instruction that employs these techniques with examples such as the early bridges.

We have also found it fairly simple to come up with interactions of the to-be-remembered information. It is important to use examples that are already familiar and meaningful to the students and then to ensure that the examples used for both the question and the answer interact. This stage could also be referred to as the relating step in the keyword and pegword methods.

After this step has been employed, the retrieving step will work in the same way as in the keyword and pegword methods. For example, when asked information about early bridges, first one thinks of "early bridges," recalls the picture that contained early bridges, and what was happening in that picture. The answer, "were made of logs and often rotted and washed away," can be easily retrieved. If the question were asked in the opposite way: "Tell me what often rotted and washed away during the early transportation era?" the answer could be retrieved just as easily by going back to the picture with the rotting wood, and retrieving "early bridges" from the interactive illustration.

We have suggested that teachers practice retrieval with students both ways, since the goal is to *learn* the information, not simply respond with rote answers. With little practice, students can really learn information.

Suggested Guidelines for Using Reconstructive Elaborations

We have developed the following guidelines that can be used to assist in adapting content area information using reconstructive elaborations. These rules serve to guide the teacher to ensure that the content has been made more familiar, meaningful, and concrete, and that a good interaction has been employed between the stimulus and response information.

Guideline one: Mimetic reconstructions. When both the stimulus (question) and response (answer) information are already familiar, meaningful, and concrete for the target population, simply provide a pictorial representation of each component interacting in one picture, image, or sentence. In this case it is mandatory that the students possess pertinent knowledge and familiarity with the information presented pictorially both in the stimulus (question) and the response (answer).

Guideline two: Symbolic reconstructions. When the stimulus (question) or response (answer) information is abstract, but partially meaningful to the students, provide a concrete instance (e.g., a symbol) in a picture, image, or sentence of that abstract concept. Then interact that symbolized reconstruction with the picture, sentence, or image of the to-be-associated information. The other piece of information to-be-associated with this symbol may need to be reconstructed either mimetically or acoustically, depending on the prior knowledge of the students.

Guideline three: Acoustic reconstructions. When the stimulus (question) or response (answer) information is totally unfamiliar to the students, the information must be reconstructed acoustically into a keyword that is familiar and sounds similar to the information to be learned. Then that acoustic reconstruction must be shown interacting with the to-be-remembered information in a picture, sentence, or image.

Guideline four: One mimetic reconstruction and one symbolic or acoustic reconstruction. When either the stimulus (question) and response (answer) information is already familiar and meaningful to the students, simply provide a pictorial (mimetic) representation of that component and have it interacting with the information from the other component in one picture, image, or sentence. The information from the second component may need to be reconstructed symbolically or acoustically, as described above.

Guideline five: Multiple reconstructions. When any new content must be remembered, any number of reconstructions can be made.

1. Determine precisely what needs to be learned.

2. Determine the level of meaningfulness and concreteness it has for the students.

3. Reconstruct each component along the continuum ranging from mimetic to symbolic to acoustic.

4. Generate an interactive picture, sentence, or image that contains all of the reconstructed components doing something together.

5. Practice retrieving the appropriate information.

In our research programs we have included many different types of reconstructed pieces of information together in single pictures. Some have included mimetic, symbolic, acoustic, and pegword reconstructions.

SUMMARY

This chapter has presented the model of reconstructive elaborations, a model used to adapt content area information into more familiar, more meaningful, and more concrete forms that students can more readily assimilate. This model incorporates the principles of elaboration; that is, any content that needs to be associated together is linked by pictorial or visual image formats. When these procedures are employed, to-be-remembered information is acquired faster and retained longer. The remaining chapters in the text provide applications of the model to various content areas.

Section Two

Applications of Mnemonic Techniques to the Curriculum

CHAPTER 5

Social Studies Applications

In geography and history classes, students are required to remember information such as the names of famous people and their particular accomplishments, or the names of places and what types of events occurred in those places, or the names of states, their capitals, and the products associated with them, or the names of particular rivers, mountains, and other natural features in specific regions of the world. Social studies content may at times be compared to novels in that stories about particular people and places are told, and students are required to recall who did what when, and how event A influenced event B. Much of the content in geography and history may not appear conceptually difficult to comprehend, but on the other hand these two areas contain an enormous amount of new information which must be remembered. Sometimes that information may be very familiar and meaningful to students, as in the case of information about their home town and home state; however, other times the information may be totally unfamiliar and not very meaningful or concrete. Some content in social studies appears very abstract for some learners, and as such, it is more difficult to picture and remember. For example, concepts such as liberty and justice may be difficult to comprehend if they are not made more concrete by providing several familiar, meaningful examples.

Geography Applications

Transportation examples. First, examine the content of the textbook or other material you want your students to learn and remember, including student and teacher texts, workbooks, teacher guides and supplementary resource materials, that was presented on transportation.

Determine what is the most important information for students to master. Then, make a list of that information similar to the example below:

TRAVEL BY LAND: EARLY ROADS

Important Stimulus Content	To-be Associated Information
1. Transportation	Different ways of travelling from place to place

2. Trace	A narrow trail used by the early pioneers for travelling
3. Corduroy Roads	Roads made by laying logs across muddy places in the trails
4. Plank Roads	Roads made of split logs that provided a flat surface (were smoother than corduroy roads)

LATER ROADS

5. Cumberland Road	A gravel road built with (National Road) government tax money; linked the East with the West (gravel roads were better than plank or corduroy roads)
6. Interstate Highways	A highway that goes between states

Next, classify the information along the "meaningfulness" dimension. Decide whether your students are familiar, partially familiar, or totally unfamiliar with the content. Once you have decided whether that content is meaningful, you can decide what the optimal mnemonic strategy should be: whether the information should be reconstructed mimetically, symbolically, or acoustically.

We determined that, for our students, stimulus items for examples 1 through 4 were all unfamiliar, but example 6 was partially familiar. Stimulus item 5, the Cumberland Road, could be developed as a symbolic reconstruction. The responses to these stimulus terms were generally familiar and meaningful. Therefore, "acoustic" reconstructions should be generated for the stimulus items 1 through 5, mimetic reconstructions for each of the responses on the to-be-associated information, and a mimetic reconstruction for stimulus item 6.

Once we made those judgments, we needed to generate the interactive elaborations in sentence, pictorial, or image format. For our teaching, we developed interactive pictures. However, for this exercise:

(1) Develop appropriate reconstructions, and

(2) interactive elaborations that connect the stimulus and response information. The words are listed again below for you. Our choices are in the appendix. Do not look ahead until you have really thought through your own choices.

Stimulus	*Reconstructions*	*Interactive Elaborations*
1. Transportation		
2. Trace		
3. Corduroy Roads		
4. Plank Roads		
5. Cumberland Road (National Road)		
6. Interstate Highway		

After comparing your answers with ours, examine whether or not your acoustic reconstructions were acoustically similar and easily pictured, and *familiar* to your own students. Also, double check to make sure that your interactive elaborations had stimulus items *doing something* with response items. Be sure your interactive elaborations do not contain extraneous information. (This might only serve to confuse the learner.) Remember, there is not a single correct response for any item; however, the guidelines for establishing effective reconstructions and good elaborations should be adhered to. If your students are familiar with some of the stimulus terms, simple mimetic reconstructions followed by good elaborations would be sufficient. For example, some middle school students may be familiar with a "plank." Therefore, those students did not need to learn the acoustic reconstruction "plant", but merely required the interactive illustration of planks on roads to establish the link that planks were used to build some of the early roads in our country.

Natural resources examples.

One particular chapter in a social studies text we used identified all the natural resources in the state of Indiana, and where they were located. Below we list the general information presented on natural resources in Indiana.

TASK:

1. Determine whether the information is familiar for your students.

2. Then, determine the type of reconstruction necessary for both stimulus and response information.

3. Finally, develop interactive elaborations containing the stimuli and responses.

Our choices are presented at the end of the chapter. Do not compare your choices with ours until you have really tried to come up with your own mnemonic pictures.

Information on Indiana Resources.

1. Indiana has both good and poor soil. The soil in the northern part of the state is good and the soil in the southern part of the state is poor.

2. Nearly 3/4 of the land in Indiana is cultivated.

3. Corn is the number one crop in Indiana.

4. Soybeans are another important crop in Indiana. Soybeans are used in making many different products. Soybeans are used to feed farm animals and house pets. Flour from soybeans is used in baby food. Oil from soybeans is used in making soap and candles.

5. Since soil is such a valuable resource, farmers use the process of crop rotation to keep the soil healthy. Crop rotation means not planting the same crop in the same place each year.

States and capitals. Most students are required to learn the names of the states and their capitals in social studies. This is an arduous task for many students because teachers often do not provide any strategies for learning or remembering the information. It also can be very frustrating and time consuming. If two acoustic reconstructions (state name and capital name) are combined in one elaboration, the learning of this information can take place more rapidly, and students enjoy the learning process.

TASK:

1. Use acoustic reconstructions for the names of all the states and the capitals and then place them in interactive illustrations. Try to complete this task by yourself. Think about the guidelines of familiarity and meaningfulness, as well as acoustic similarity.

2. Develop elaborations in which the keyword for the state is doing something with the keyword for the capital. Here is the list: You can compare your choices with ours in the Appendix.

State	Capital
Alabama	Montgomery
Alaska	Juneau
Arkansas	Little Rock
Arizona	Phoenix
California	Sacramento
Colorado	Denver
Connecticut	Hartford
Delaware	Dover
Florida	Tallahassee
Georgia	Atlanta

Hawaii	Honolulu
Idaho	Boise
Illinois	Springfield
Indiana	Indianapolis
Iowa	Des Moines
Kansas	Topeka
Kentucky	Frankfort
Louisiana	Baton Rouge
Maine	Augusta
Maryland	Annapolis
Massachusetts	Boston
Michigan	Lansing
Minnesota	St. Paul
Missouri	Jefferson City
Mississippi	Jackson
Montana	Helena
Nebraska	Lincoln
Nevada	Carson City
New Hampshire	Concord
New Jersey	Trenton
New Mexico	Santa Fe
New York	Albany
North Carolina	Raleigh
North Dakota	Bismark
Ohio	Columbus
Oklahoma	Oklahoma City
Oregon	Salem
Pennsylvania	Harrisburg
Rhode Island	Providence
South Carolina	Columbia
South Dakota	Pierre
Tennessee	Nashville
Texas	Austin
Utah	Salt Lake City
Vermont	Montpelier
Virginia	Richmond
Washington	Olympia
West Virginia	Charleston
Wisconsin	Madison
Wyoming	Cheyenne

History Examples

Most students enroll in U.S. History classes several times throughout their school years. One might think, then, that our students graduate from high school as experts in the history of the United States. On the contrary, many students cannot even identify the half-century in which the Civil War took place, let alone tell you the accomplishments of many of the important figures throughout our country's history. This lack of basic knowledge has been reported by E. D. Hirsch Jr. in his book *Cultural Literacy: What Every American Needs to Know*. Hirsch documented that students do not learn and remember basic information regarding our common heritage. Below are some examples of how you can improve your students' recall of important historical concepts and events. They can be used with a variety of other similar topics.

Presidents of the United States. A task that is often required is to learn the names and orders of the presidents of the United States, an arduous task for many students. Using adaptations described in the pegword chapter, students have been much more successful at learning the proper sequence of the presidents.

TASK: Make your own mnemonic list of the order of the presidents of the United States. Use keywords for reconstructing the presidents' names, and pegwords for determining the order of their presidency. This keyword-pegword strategy is similar to the one used for learning the hardness levels of minerals, as discussed in Chapter 3.

Since there are more than ten presidents, you need an additional strategy to indicate the *decade* of number the pegword represents; for example: that a particular president is the 3rd, rather than the 13th or 23rd. To do this, use a seasonal *method of loci* to represent the decade of numbers. For instance, a *spring garden* scene represents the numbers 1-10; a *summer beach* scene represents the 2nd decade, numbers 11-20; and so on. Some have used the points on a compass (e.g., North, South, East, and West) as loci.

What is most important is that you adhere to the guidelines and that the information is made into a more meaningful memorable form, so that recall is facilitated. Don't forget to have a good elaboration in which the keyword for the president's name is doing something with the pegword for the number (in a particular loci or decade).

Mnemonic strategies for all U.S. Presidents are given in the Appendix. This is a very complicated strategy, however, and when teaching it, be sure to allow sufficient time for students to learn to use it. At first, it may be helpful to provide students with practice retrieving numbers given the pegword and season [e.g., "What number does a *bun* on a *summer beach* stand for?" (11) "A *tree* in a *fall Thanksgiving dinner?"*(23) "A *hive* on a *winter snowman?"*(35)]. Then, after the keywords and presidents' names have been thoroughly practiced, students may have less difficulty retrieving the answers. Good luck and keep on trying, even if it seems hard. The technique becomes much easier with practice. Here is the list:

Number	President	Keyword	Pegword	Loci	Elaboration
1.	George Washington				
2.	John Adams				
3.	Thomas Jefferson				
4.	James Madison				
5.	James Monroe				
6.	John Quincy Adams				
7.	Andrew Jackson				
8.	Martin Van Buren				
9.	William H. Harrison				
10.	John Tyler				
11.	James K. Polk				
12.	Zachary Taylor				
13.	Millard Fillmore				
14.	Franklin Pierce				
15.	James Buchanan				
16.	Abraham Lincoln				
17.	Andrew Johnson				
18.	Ulysses S. Grant				
19.	Rutherford B. Hayes				
20.	James A. Garfield				
21.	Chester A. Arthur				
22.	Grover Cleveland				
23.	William McKinley				
24.	Theodore Roosevelt				
25.	William H. Taft				
26.	Woodrow Wilson				
27.	Warren G. Harding				
28.	Calvin Coolidge				
29.	Herbert C. Hoover				
30.	Franklin D. Roosevelt				
31.	Harry S. Truman				
32.	Dwight D. Eisenhower				
33.	John F. Kennedy				
34.	Lyndon B. Johnson				
35.	Richard M. Nixon				
36.	Gerald R. Ford				
37.	James E. Carter				
38.	Ronald Reagan				
39.	George Bush				

Learning Historic Facts

Students take U.S. History in the fifth, eighth, and eleventh grades, with occasional repetitions occurring even before grade five, as well as in between the grades listed. Consequently, one might think that our students graduate from high school knowing the history of the United States. On the contrary; it has been widely reported that many of our students cannot even identify the half-century in which the Civil War took place, let alone tell you the accomplishments of many of the important figures in our country's history. Hirsch (1987) has carefully documented that students in our educational system are not learning basic information regarding our common heritage.

Our analysis of U.S. history textbooks at the various grade levels indicates that a common core of information is presented in the textbooks written for the fifth, eighth, and eleventh grades. What sometimes varies is the amount of details supplied about different events, and the difficulty of vocabulary used to describe the particular events and people.

By using our reconstructive elaborations model, students can learn a significant amount of information in a short period of time. If students can master the essence of an era, as well as learn the names, places, and major events rapidly, they will probably be *better able to* participate in discussions about those people, places, and events.

The American Revolution. In studying information about the American Revolutionary War, the content can be subdivided using the following major headings to organize the sequence of events:

I. Breaking with Britain
- A. Commander General George Washington
- B. Arnold captures Fort Ticonderoga
- C. Battle of Bunker Hill
- D. Montgomery captures Montreal
- E. General Howe forced to leave Boston Harbor

II. Moving Toward Independence
- A. Patriots versus Loyalists
- B. Patriots' victory at Moore's Creek Bridge
- C. Thomas Paine's "Common Sense"
- D. The Declaration of Independence
- E. Philadelphia—first Capitol

III. Victories and defeats
- A. British attack Long Island
- B. Washington crosses the Delaware
- C. Washington captures Trenton

D. Burgoyne surrenders at Saratoga

E. British victory at Brandywine Creek

F. George Washington at Valley Forge

IV. Final Independence

A. Treaty of Alliance

B. John Paul Jones

C. George Rogers Clark

D. Guerrilla warfare

E. Cornwallis surrenders at Yorktown

F. Second Treaty of Paris

This, of course, is not the only way to organize the information, nor is every major event in the Revolutionary War included. This outline captures several major events as they have been covered in many U.S. history textbooks.

This outline should be supplemented with teacher materials that include information to be learned under each major subheading on the outline and, most importantly, *a strategy for remembering that information*. Overhead transparencies, which graphically display the mnemonic illustrations for students, can be included. Student workbooks that reiterate the information and that include a copy of the mnemonic illustration, can also be used. Finally, student practice and worksheet activities can be developed to provide opportunities for retrieving the strategic information, and the content.

These materials should be supplemented with information presented in textbooks, classroom discussions, films, extra resource activities, and any other sources of relevant information pertaining to the American Revolutionary War.

In developing the mnemonic strategies we used the reconstructive elaborations model and the guidelines. We attempted to organize the content in terms of stimulus (question) and response information, and then determined whether or not the information is familiar and meaningful, abstract and partially familiar, or totally unfamiliar to the students prior to the actual strategy development.

TASK: Use the outline presented above to determine the level of familiarity of the information for your students. We list additional information for the second section of the outline below. Then based upon that knowledge, select the appropriate reconstructive elaboration strategy and actually develop a good interactive elaboration. You can compare your strategies with those we developed. Remember, it is OK for your strategy to be different from ours, as long as it meets the criteria of meaningfulness, familiarity, acoustic similarity, and interactive elaborations.

The following sample lesson on the Revolutionary War is based on Section II of the outline presented above.

A SAMPLE REVOLUTIONARY WAR LESSON

Teacher: We have been studying information about the beginning of the American Revolutionary War. We have covered the early years of that conflict, which we called "The Break with Britain." Before we go on, let's review some of that information. Who can tell me about Benedict Arnold and Fort Ticonderoga? [Reviews previous information].

Statement of Lesson Objective. Today we are going to learn about the next part of the Revolutionary War, a part we call "Moving Toward Independence." After we learn the important information, we will view a film strip on this part of the Revolutionary War and discuss it.

Presentation of New Information. Teacher: During the early years of the Revolutionary War, some colonists remained loyal to the British. They were called *Loyalists* or Tories. The Loyalists wanted to stay a colony of the British. They did not want independence from Britain.

Figure 5.1 Loyalists (loyal) = Loyal to the British

[Shows picture on overhead projector]. Think of this picture of the Loyalists looking at the royal king of England while they are saying: "We are loyal (for Loyalists) to the royal king of England". This will help remind you that the loyalists were the colonists who remained loyal to the British. Susan, what does **loyalist** mean?

The **Patriots** were the colonists who wanted independence from the British. The Patriots wanted to become an independent country.

[Shows picture on overhead projector]. To represent the Patriots, we are going to use the New England Patriots football team. Think of this picture of the New England Patriots football team (for Patriots) pushing the British king down. The Patriots are saying: "Down with the King! We want independence!" This will help you remember that the Patriots were the colonists who wanted independence from the British. Who can tell me who the Patriots were?

Many Loyalists lived in North and South Carolina. These Loyalists started to march to Wilmington to help the British. But the Patriots stopped the Loyalists on their way and defeated them at the *Battle of Moore's Creek Bridge*.

[Shows picture on overhead projector]. We are going to think of the word **more** to help us remember Moore's Creek Bridge. Think of this picture of the New England Patriots (for Patriots) sending *more* Patriots over Moore's Creek Bridge while they are chasing the Loyalists (loyal to the royal king) away. The Patriots are saying:

Figure 5.2 Battle of Moore's (more) Creek Bridge = Patriots (New England Patriots) Defeated Loyalists (loyal)

"Send *more* Patriots over Moore's Creek Bridge." While the royal Loyalists are saying: "Help! We are loyal to the royal King", as they ran away from the Patriots at Moore's Creek Bridge. This will help you remember that the Patriots defeated the Loyalists at Moore's Creek Bridge. Jeremy, what happened at Moore's Creek Bridge?

Thomas Paine was a poor young writer. He arrived in America less than a year after fighting had started between the American colonies and Britain. In January 1776, Paine published a pamphlet called *Common Sense*. In the pamphlet, Paine stated that it was only common sense for the Colonists to declare their independence from Britain. It convinced many doubtful men and women that independence from Great Britain was proper.

[Shows picture on overhead projector]. We will use *pain* as a keyword for Thomas Paine. Think of this picture of Thomas Paine sitting at a desk writing and saying: "I've got a pain (for T. Paine) from writing!" A woman replies: "If you had *common sense* you'd stop writing." Also notice the sign that says: "Common Sense: Fight the British." This will help you remember that Thomas Paine wrote *Common Sense* and urged all Americans to declare their independence from Britain. Who can tell me about Thomas Paine?

Philadelphia was the first capitol of the United States. It was America's largest city and the meeting place of the Continental Congress.

[Shows picture on overhead projector]. Let's use the word **bell**

Figure 5.3 Thomas Paine (pain) Wrote "Common Sense"

as a keyword for Philadelphia. This is a short keyword for a long name, but think of the "bell" as sounding like "del," the accented syllable in Philadelphia. Think of this picture of the Liberty Bell sitting in front of the Capitol Building with a sign that says: Philadelphia: 1st Capitol of the U.S." This will help you remember that Philadelphia was the first capitol of the U.S. and the meeting place of the Second Continental Congress.

On June 7, 1776, the Second Continental Congress said, "These united colonies ought to be free and independent states." For over a month the Continental Congress debated this move. All of the delegates finally approved the *Declaration of Independence* on July 4, 1776, in Philadelphia. It was America's largest city and the meeting place of the Continental Congress.

[Shows picture on overhead projector]. Let's use **declare** as a keyword for Declaration of Independence. Think of this picture of two New England Patriots (for Patriots) standing next to the Liberty Bell (for Philadelphia) holding a sign that says: "Declaration of Independence". Notice that one Patriot is saying: "We declare (for Declaration of Independence) we are independent from Britain." Notice the number 76 is on the Patriots' shirts. This will help you remember the Declaration of Independence was signed in Philadelphia on July 4, 1776.

Guided Practice Now, let's go over this information without the pictures. I'll call on the class to answer together, or individuals one at a time. [Reviews information].

Independent Practice I will now show you a brief film strip that covers the events we learned about today. I will hand out a worksheet that you can fill out yourselves as you watch the film strip [hands out worksheets].

Evaluation Now I'll give you a brief quiz on the information we covered.

Additional history examples

The following information uses combinations of the various techniques we have presented.

TASK: Use the textual information to determine, first, the important information to **be learned,** the **level of meaningfulness** and familiarity of that information for your students, and finally, the **type of reconstructive elaboration** necessary to facilitate your students' learning the information. Turn to the appendix to check your answers.

World War I

1. In 1914 when World War I was just beginning in Europe, there were two major alliances. Different groups of countries in Europe formed alliances with each other. This means they agreed not to fight each other, and to defend each other from attacks by countries outside their own alliance or grouping.

2. One of the two major alliances in Europe was called the Central Powers. The countries in the Central Powers were Turkey, Austria-Hungary, and Germany.

3. The other major alliance was called the Allied Powers. The countries in the Allied Powers were France, Italy, Russia, and England.

SUMMARY

The information presented in this chapter illustrates how you can use the mnemonic techniques to help improve your students' recall of social studies information. Our research findings indicate that if you develop strategies like these you will not only enjoy it, but your students will enjoy learning more and perform better on their tests.

CHAPTER 6

Applications of Mnemonic Techniques to Science Topics

As in social studies, science is an area in which many students experience much frustration and disappointment. There are many causes for this frustration. Although science itself is a fascinating subject, many students may fail to become interested because they fail to learn and remember key concepts and vocabulary. Without this foundation, more advanced learning and meaningful applications are impossible. In other cases, the content may be too complex or abstract for some students to readily grasp. Many advocates of science education have stressed the importance of experiment and discovery in science learning. Nevertheless, many key concepts and vocabulary must first be learned to make later experiment and discovery meaningful.

Mnemonic techniques can be very effective in science teaching, since they help make complex content simpler, abstractions more concrete, and seemingly meaningless information more meaningful.

This section covers procedures using mnemonic techniques for teaching science content. In general, the model of "reconstructive elaborations," described in the previous chapter, is used. We offer three areas of applications: life science, earth history, and geology.

Life Science

Life science, as typically taught, has much to do with the classification, organization, and description of living things. Therefore, much instruction in life science has to do with learning characteristics and taxonomies. This type of learning easily lends itself to mnemonic instruction.

Vertebrates. The study of vertebrates is a relatively easy unit in life science, because students usually are familiar with many of the relevant concepts. In fact, most students are familiar with what a "backbone" is, although they may not know the meaning of the word "vertebrate." In this case, a keyword strategy is helpful in teaching this verbal label for an already-familiar concept.

"Dirt" can be used as a keyword for "vertebrate" because it sounds like the first syllable of vertebrate and can be pictured (e.g., a dirt pile). A picture then can show a backbone (or a vertebrate animal with an obvious backbone) sticking out of a pile of dirt, to help students remember this definition of vertebrate.

There are five major divisions of vertebrates: Amphibians, Fish, Reptiles, Birds, and Mammals. Using the model of reconstructive elaborations described in the previous chapter, you can see that two of the five, fish and birds are almost certainly familiar to students. Therefore, fish and birds can be shown in *mimetic* or representational pictures, and important concrete attributes, such as scales, fins, and feathers, can be portrayed within these mimetic pictures.

Reptiles are also familiar to many students. However, many other students may not know what reptiles are, or they may not know all the different types of reptiles, such as snakes, lizards, turtles, and crocodilians. If reptiles are as familiar to students as birds and fish, they can be presented in a mimetic picture. If they are less familiar, a keyword elaboration will be helpful. In this case, the word "tiles" could be a good keyword for reptiles, because it sounds like the second syllable for reptiles, and can be pictured. A picture depicting reptiles interacting with tiles, e.g., a picture of snakes, lizards, turtles, and crocodilians sitting on tiles, or with tiles for scales, or both, could be effective.

TASK:(1) Think of keywords for the remaining, unfamiliar (to students) types of vertebrates:

Name	*Keyword*	*Picture*
Amphibian		
Mammal		

(2) Think of an interactive picture to present amphibians and mammals.

Possible keywords could be "bib" for amphibian (*amplifier* may also be good), and "camel" for mammal. "Bib" is an acceptable keyword because, although a short keyword for a long word, bib sounds very much like the accented second syllable of amphibian. Camel is a particularly good keyword because a camel *is* a mammal.

Organization. Much of life science instruction involves teaching which of several types of plants or animals go together. With respect to the *vertebrates* examples, above, students may be required to "Name the five types of vertebrates." Once the names of these animals have become familiar, a first-letter strategy is appropriate. The first letters of the five vertebrates can not be combined to make a "real" word, but together they do form the acronym (suggested by Roy Halleran), "FARM-B." Now, FARM-B does not convey any particular meaning to us, other than, say, an unusual name for a farm;

nevertheless, with a little practice this can become a very effective mnemonic for retrieving fish, amphibian, reptile, mammal, bird. To integrate this idea with the concept "vertebrate," place a picture of each animal on a pile of *dirt* (keyword for vertebrate). Also, to reinforce the keywords in the acoustically transformed animal names, show the amphibian with a *bib*, the reptile on *tiles*, and a camel for the *mammal*.

Attributes. Also important to life sciences is the teaching of specific attributes, or characteristics, associated with particular types of plants or animals. In the vertebrates examples above, you can teach some attributes associated with each of the types of vertebrates. One important attribute is whether a particular type of vertebrate is warm-blooded or cold-blooded. You can use **warm** or **cold** scenes to picture the animals in symbolic reconstructions for warm-blooded or cold blooded. For example, to show that birds are warm-blooded, depict a bird in a warm, sunny scene; to show that reptiles are cold-blooded, you can depict reptiles in a cold, snowy scene.

But there is a complication. Reptiles and amphibians do not really exist (in a non-dormant state) in cold snowy scenes. This picture presents potentially confusing information. Instead, you may choose to depict your reptiles and amphibians looking cold and uncomfortable in their scenes, rather than playing and having fun in the snow. It is then easier to teach that cold-blooded animals cannot function in the cold. This picture is really a way of enforcing that they

Figure 6.1 Types of Vertebrates = Fish, Amphibians (bib), Reptiles (tiles), Mammals (camel), and Birds (FARM - B)

are cold-blooded.

You can teach several attributes with one picture of mammals. First, that mammals are warm-blooded; second, that they include cats, dogs, and people; third, that they have hair or fur on their bodies; fourth, that the young are fed milk by their mothers. These attributes can be integrated into one picture with several different mnemonic reconstructions. First, use the *camel* keyword by providing a train of three camels in a *hot, sunny,* desert scene, a symbolic reconstruction for *warm-blooded,* and include a cat, a dog, and a person riding the camels to show different kinds of mammals. All these animals can be shown with *hair* or *fur,* to depict that attribute of mammals. Finally, you can show the cat, dog, and person as *young* individuals depicting them *drinking milk.* In one picture, you can teach that mammals are warm-blooded, include cats, dogs, and people, have hair or fur, and that the young drink milk.

Let's try an example with natural history, and this time you try to design the mnemonic pictures. This example comes from a study conducted by ourselves and Debra Tolfa Veit, in which students were taught, among other things, attributes of several dinosaurs. For each of these dinosaurs, students were expected to state whether they were meat-eaters (carnivorous) or plant-eaters (herbivorous); whether they came from the early (Triassic), middle (Jurassic), or late (Cretaceous) period of the Mesozoic era; and one attribute specific to each dinosaur. Below we list dinosaur names and attributes. Choose the

Figure 6.2 Attributes of Mammals (camel) = fur, warm-blooded (sun), young drink milk

mnemonic strategies for teaching this information. Later, compare
your choices with those in the Appendix.

Name	Keyword	Eats	Period	Specific	Strategy
Allosaurus		Meat	Middle	Ran fast as a man.	
Brachiosaurus		Plants	Middle	Largest dinosaur.	
Spinosaurus		Meat	Late	Sail on back.	
Coelophysus		Meat	Early	Cared for young.	
Tyrannosaurus		Meat	Late	Hunted in groups.	
Stegosaurus		Plants	Middle	Brain size of walnut.	
Plateosaurus		Plants	Early	Walked on four legs.	
Ankylosaurus		Plants	Late	Used tail for club.	

More examples. Here are some examples of life science content,
involving invertebrate animals. See if you can develop strategies for
recalling this information, and test yourself on your recall. Then, turn
to the appendix and compare your reconstructions with ours.

Name	Keyword	Attribute	Strategy
Mollusk		Includes clams and snails. Eaten by people.	
Arthropods		Includes crabs and lobsters.	
Insects		Have six legs.	
Trichina		Roundworm parasite found in undercooked pork which causes diseases in people.	
Earthworm		Segmented body, many hearts, lives in the earth.	
Radial Symmetry		Structural condition in which identical body parts extend out from the center, as in a starfish.	

TASK: Learning the classification system for plants and animals.
(Remember that this is *ordered* information). Once you have developed a mnemonic system for teaching this information, compare
your strategies with the ones in the appendix.

1. Kingdom

2. Phylum

3. Class

4. Order

5. Family

6. Genus

7. Species

Earth History

Earth history involves the learning of different chronological periods, their orders, and attributes associated with these different periods. These attributes include types of plant and animal life (if any), and conditions of the land and seas.

Earth history also requires novel vocabulary words which can be taught using the keyword method. Fossil, for example, means any evidence of past life taken from rock. This word can be taught via the keyword *faucet*, and an interactive picture of *fossils* coming out of a *faucet*.

Other vocabulary words from earth history are more complex and may be more effectively taught by teaching the root words and then practicing them in their various combinations. For example, consider such words as paleontology, paleozoic, mesozoic, and cenozoic. These words share some common roots, which, once learned, can be combined and recombined. Since all these words are likely to be unfamiliar to learners, acoustic reconstructions via the keyword method are appropriate.

TASK: Create keywords and interactive strategies for the following roots:

Root Word	Keyword	Definition	Strategy
paleo-		old	
-ology		study of	
zoo-		animals	
meso-		middle	
ceno-		new	

When you have completed this table, compare your choices with the ones in the appendix.

Attributes. Develop strategies for recalling attributes associated with each of three eras:

Era	Keyword	Attributes	Strategy
Paleozoic		Shallow oceans, high mountains, first plants, first fish, scorpions.	
Mesozoic		Dinosaurs, extinction of dinosaurs, first birds.	
Cenozoic		Mammals, first humans, ice ages.	

Our choices are given in the Appendix.

Geology

More minerals. In the Chapter 3, strategies for remembering minerals and their associated hardness levels were described. Below we list more minerals, their hardness levels, colors, and common use. Develop strategies for remembering these attributes, then check the appendix for our own strategies. [Chapter 3 can be used for a review].

Name	Keyword	Hardness	Color	Use	Strategy
Talc		1	White	Powder	
Crocoite		2	Orange	Displays	
Calcite		3	Gray	Steel	
Wolframite		4	Black	Light Bulbs	
Apatite		5	Brown	Fertilizer	
Pyrite		6	Yellow	Acid	
Quartz		7	Pink	Radios	
Beryl		8	Green	Alloy	
Corundum		9	Red	Jewelry	

Rocks. Three types of rock are generally given as *igneous*, *metamorphic*, and *sedimentary*. **Igneous rock** comes from molten or volcanic rock; **metamorphic rock** is rock which has changed from heat and pressure; and **sedimentary rock** is rock which is made of tiny rock particles which have settled in oceans or lakes. To teach this information, you could use the keywords "pig" for igneous, "met-a-dwarf" for metamorphic, and "settle" for sedimentary. Then create interactive pictures of pigs coming out of a volcano and turning into rock; someone who "met a dwarf" who was using heat and pressure to make metamorphic rock; and sand and other particles in the sea "settling" to form sedimentary rock.

It is also important to teach different kinds of igneous, metamorphic, and sedimentary rock. See if you can come up with strategies to teach three examples each of these types of rock, then check your choices with those at the end of the chapter.

Name	Examples	Strategies
Igneous	basalt	
	granite	
	olivine	
Metamorphic	marble	
	quartz	
	slate	
Sedimentary	sandstone	
	limestone	
	shale	

A GEOLOGY LESSON USING MNEMONIC TECHNIQUES

Review of Previous Information Teacher: We have been learning about the history of the Earth. Let's review what we have learned so far. [Reviews previous content].

Statement of Lesson Objective Today, we're going to learn about the three sections of the earth. We will learn their names and what they are composed of.

Presentation of New Information. Earth has an internal *core* of iron and nickel, which is covered by a *mantle* of solid rock. Finally, the earth is covered by a *crust*, consisting of the continents and ocean floors which cover the earth's surface.

Let's use some keywords to remember the names of each section of the earth. For *core*, let's use an apple core (keyword for core) made up of *irons* and *nickels* (keywords for iron and nickel). [Shows picture]. This picture shows an apple core made of irons and nickels. This will help us remember that the Earth's core is made of iron and nickel. What is it made of, Marty? How can you remember that?

For mantle, we can use a *man* (keyword for mantle) made of *solid rock* [Shows picture]. Look of this picture of a man made of solid rock. What is the Earth's mantle made of, Cindy? How do you remember that?

Finally, for *crust*, we can use *crusts of bread* (keyword for crust)

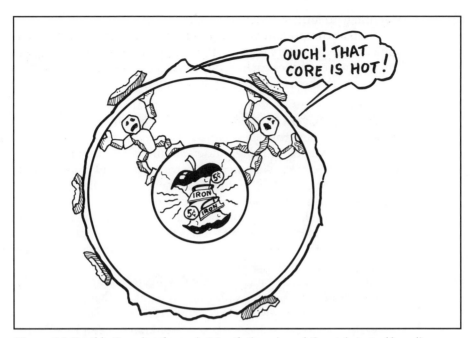

Figure 6.3 Earth's Core (apple core), Mantle (man), and Crust (crust of bread)

on the mountains and floating in the earth's oceans. [Shows picture]. Remember this picture of crusts of bread on the earth's mountains and oceans. This will help you remember that the Earth's crust is the mountains and ocean floors. What is the Earth's crust? How can you remember that?

Now, we know what the core, mantle, and crust are made of. However, it is also important to learn *where* in the earth these sections are. [Shows picture]. Therefore, using the keywords we used before, look at this picture of the earth with an *apple core* at the center, and *rock men* standing on the core, holding up the crust of the earth, which has bread crusts floating on it. You can see that the rock men are receiving hot feet from the core, and saying, "Ouch! That core is hot!" That will help you remember that the core is very hot.

Guided Practice. So, who can explain what the three parts of the Earth are? [Reviews information covered in the lesson].

Independent Practice. Now I'm going to ask you to take out a pencil and a piece of paper and draw the three sections of the earth. Make sure you label each and write what each is made of. If you need help, you can raise your hand and ask me, or ask your neighbor to help you.

Evaluation. Now clear your desks, take out a pencil and paper, and we'll see how much you learned today [gives quiz].

FINAL CONSIDERATIONS

In these two chapters, we have shown that much of the commonly taught information in social studies and science can be adapted to mnemonic instruction using the model of reconstructive elaborations. Some examples were given from social studies and science content often covered in school. However, virtually any social studies or science content can be adapted to mnemonic instruction to the benefit of students' learning, understanding, and retention of this information. Subjects such as U.S. Government and Constitution, world history, anatomy, matter and energy, and chemistry lend themselves readily to mnemonic adaptation.

We re-emphasize that mnemonic techniques are ideal for helping students learn fundamental classifications, concepts, vocabulary, and discriminations. This learning can be reinforced by various experiences. For instance, students who have learned important classifications and attributes of minerals will probably benefit greatly from experiencing actual displays of minerals, either from school collections, field trips to museums or quarries, or from media such as film strips or videotape. In such cases, their knowledge and curiosity will probably be much greater because the important verbal information is now familiar to them. Students who have learned important new concepts and terminology can be expected to feel more a part of such experiences, as with the new knowledge comes a greater personal investment. Under such circumstances, mnemonic instruction can help to foster personal interest in the study of social studies and science and the other subject areas these techniques can be used to learn.

CHAPTER 7

Basic Skills:
Reading and Mathematics

Mnemonic techniques also can be applied in the basic skills areas, such as reading, math, spelling, and language arts. This chapter describes some applications.

The function of mnemonics in basic skills areas is the same as in other areas: to improve initial associations through enhancing familiarity, meaningfulness, and concreteness. Associative learning is important in the basic skills areas, and this is the type of learning tasks which can be most easily adapted to mnemonic instruction. Some examples of this, in different skill areas, are provided below.

READING

Many people look at reading as a unitary skill because skilled readers simply read without being particularly aware of the separate steps they are executing. However, reading is a complex set of skills including rules and procedures which must be learned. Reading skills must be practiced over and over until they become *automatic*.

A first step in learning to read is learning the sound-symbol relationships. Such learning is *associative*; it is similar, psychologically, to the learning tasks described earlier, and can be facilitated by mnemonic reconstructions.

Pictures to enhance learning of letter sounds are often seen in classrooms. They usually take the form of a letter paired with a picture of an object whose first letter represents the sound of the letter displayed, such as *a* = [picture of an apple]. While such pictures do provide information on the appropriate letter sound, they are not truly mnemonic because they do not provide an effective connection between the symbol and the sound that it represents. In other words, there is no direct link between the "a" symbol and the picture of the apple. In fact, research has shown that such pictures are not particularly effective in improving recall of the letter sound.

However, effective retrieval links between letters and sounds can be developed, and research has shown that these pictured links can be very effective in teaching letter sounds. For example, instead of showing the letter "a" *next to* a picture of an apple, teachers can show pictures of the letter "a" *integrated within* a picture of an apple. Additionally, an "s" can be made to look like a snake, or, a "g" can be integrated into a picture of glasses:

Remember, the letter must form an integral part of the picture. If it is simply placed within the picture (for example, an "a" printed on an apple, or a "g" printed on a pair of glasses), the picture will not be as effective. But, if the letters form a necessary part of the picture, it will be very difficult to remember the letter without thinking of the picture which goes with it. While working at the Mt. Holyoke College Learning Disabilities Center, Barbara Jones taught one of us (MAM) how to use these procedures for teaching students the vowel sounds. Now, you try to create mnemonic pictures for the 23 remaining letters.

Automaticity and Stages of Learning

It is critically important that reading skills become *automatic*, that students recognize letters, words, or even phrases immediately without thinking. As long as the student has to think back to pictures to remember the sounds of letters, the higher level tasks of sound blending, fluency, and comprehension, will be difficult. Nevertheless, a slower pace in initial acquisition is acceptable to serve as a basis for later fluency. In our book, *Effective Instruction for Special Education*, we argue that learning typically proceeds in stages. Special or remedial education teachers should pay particular attention to the stage of learning. At the initial *acquisition* stage, students first learn fundamental associations necessary for learning a new skill or content domain. Mnemonic instruction is particularly helpful at this stage.

Once relevant associations have been acquired, one seeks a level of *automaticity*, immediate knowledge without conscious thinking or effort. To accomplish this goal, fast-paced drill and practice are usually helpful to achieve fluency. If information is forgotten during fluency instruction, the acquisition learning strategies should be reviewed. Otherwise, students should be reinforced for fast, fluent

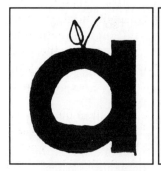

Figure 7.1 Mnemonic "a"   *Figure 7.2 Mnemonic "s"*   *Figure 7.3 Mnemonic "g"*

responding, whether reading, writing, spelling, or performing computations.

Students are taught to become fluent so that the next stage, *application*, can be achieved. During this stage of instruction, students are given opportunities to independently apply what they have learned with a wide variety of materials. Finally, in many cases it is necessary for students to *generalize* meanings or uses for what they have learned to novel circumstances.

If you view learning as passing through these four stages, you can easily see that mnemonic instruction in the basic skill areas is most useful at the initial acquisition stage, when slower responding is acceptable. Once associations have been made firmly (for example, letter sounds), practice should be given to achieve faster responding. With practice, students' responses become automatic; they no longer rely exclusively on mnemonic pictures to retrieve the necessary information. However, they will have benefited greatly from the initial "boost" in their learning!

SPELLING

Students should be taught to spell as they are taught to read. At the earliest stages, students can rely in part on the "mnemonics for phonics" described above. Later, different techniques may be helpful.

In Chapter 2, a first letter strategy for learning and remembering the spelling of long and difficult words was described. This method could soon prove to be very cumbersome. For learning and recalling the spellings of a variety of difficult words, there is a more effective strategy.

If students are familiar with sound-symbol relationships, they should be able to render at least a phonetic spelling of any word they are able to read. However, an enormous number of English words are spelled in ways that openly violate spelling or phonic rules. It is with those irregular or arbitrary associations that mnemonic instruction is most effective. The mnemonic technique provides a "reason" why a word should be spelled a certain way, when in reality no clear reason exists. Many people are already familiar with some of these mnemonics. One popular mnemonic teaches the distinction in the spellings of the homonyms principal and principle: "A principal is your pal; a principle is a rule."

An Example: Consider the word *early*. The "r" makes the conventional "r" sound, and "ly" is a regular suffix, which also spells as it sounds. However, why is "ea" used to make the initial vowel sound? According to the phonics rules, "ea" should be pronounced as long "e" ("when two vowels go walking, the first does the talking"), which is not the case in this instance. In fact, the spelling more accurately *should* be i̲rly.

What is needed is an elaboration which would help remind learners of the "ea" in the spelling of "early." One spelling that may be known to students is the spelling of *ear*. *Ear* is spelled phonetically regularly, and comprises the first three (and most difficult) letters of "early." Students should be reminded of the "ear" in "early" with an elaborative sentence which links the critical components of to-be-associated information. In the present example, a good elaborative sentence could be, "The alarm clock rang in his *ear early* in the morning." Students who remember this sentence should also remember that "ear" is a part of "early."

Harry Shefter, in his book, *Six Minutes a Day to Perfect Spelling*, provides several different examples of this spelling mnemonic. One example is a strategy for remembering the spelling of the word "cemetery." In most cases, cemetery is misspelled because students forget which vowels are included in the word. Shefter recommends use of the following mnemonic sentence: "She screamed E-E-E as she walked by the cemetery." A concrete picture of this elaborative sentence, as shown below, could help make the strategy more memorable.

Here are some more examples of words which contain unusual or arbitrary spellings. See if you can come up with spelling mnemonics to help students remember how to spell these words. Remember,

Figure 7.4 Mnemonic Spelling Strategy: "She Screamed `E-E-E' as She Walked by the Cemetery"

first think of the part of the word that is likely to be forgotten (like the "ea" in early). Next, think of a word that is spelled like this word or word part. Finally, create an elaborative sentence that will connect the two parts. When you have finished, compare your choices with those given in the appendix.

Spelling Word	*Strategy*
answer	
believe	
break	
built	
business	
does	
forty	
grammar	
minute	
none	
piece	
whole	
women	

MATHEMATICS

The ultimate goal of mathematics is to enable students to reason with numbers, and all teaching of mathematics should contribute in some way to this end. Nevertheless, it cannot be denied that a good memory is necessary for effective functioning in mathematics. This doesn't mean just memorizing math facts and formulae (although it is important to know these); it also means remembering the names of important concepts, and the sequence of important operations in mathematics. In many of these cases, mnemonic techniques can be helpful. Some examples are given below.

Mathematics Vocabulary

Although mathematics is the study of abstract numbers, many students are confused by the vocabulary employed to represent many abstract math concepts. Much of this vocabulary can be taught mnemonically, using the keyword procedures described in Chapter 2. For example, many students may confuse *multiplier* and *multiplicand*. Since both words have the same first five letters, the discrimination must be made at the end of the word. In this case, *pliers* could be a good keyword for *multiplier*, and *hand* could be a good keyword for *multiplicand*. Pictures could then be constructed of *pliers* forming the multiplication sign, next to the multi<u>plier</u>, and the multiplicand written on (or by) a *hand*. Likewise, for a division problem, the di<u>visor</u> could be wearing a *visor*, the divi<u>den</u>d could be *in* the *den* (i.e., inside the division lines), and the *quotient* could be written in *quotation* marks. Once initial concepts have been mastered, students can be taught their place within different formats.

Touch Math

One system that employs many of the mnemonic principles described here that may be of value in several math operations has been described by Jan Bullock, Sandy Pierce, Libby McClellan, and Lyn Strand, and referred to as *Touch Math*. Essentially, Touch Math presents dots, representing quantity, on each number, which can later be imaged. For instance, the number one has one dot in the middle, two has two dots, and so on up to five. The dots are integrated within the shape of the numbers, similar in a way to the phonetic mnemonics described above. For numbers six through nine, *double touches* are used. These are dots with circles around them, signifying the value "2." The number six has 3 double touches, seven has three double and a *single* touch, eight has four double touches, and nine has four double and one single touch. Due to the way these indicators have been integrated into the numbers, they are easy for students to learn and remember. Additional knowledge of place value can teach students to remember values higher than nine.

Touch math procedures have been recommended for addition, subtraction, multiplication, and division, and it seems likely that these procedures could be very helpful, especially for addition and subtraction. For instance, the dots provide a type of integrated *number line*, on which students can count values. Given enough practice, it seems likely these facts will become more automatic.

Multiplication and division require counting by the number values (that is, by 3's, 4's, 5's, etc.) and may require additional practice. Nevertheless, students who have difficulty acquiring basic facts in math may find Touch Math useful.

Pegword Systems

Multiplication tables can present particular difficulties for some students. For some, the amount of facts to be learned seems endless; no matter how many are learned, there are many more to take their place. Sometimes it is helpful to point out how many facts have been learned; often it is more than students would have guessed. For example, students knowing addition facts and relevant concepts already know the 0, 1, and 2 tables. Many students can count by 5's and therefore have this table available to them.

A simple strategy can show the student how to compute 9's tables: Hold your ten fingers out in front of you, palms down. Count whatever number you wish to multiply 9 by, from left to right, on your fingers. Put that finger down. The number of fingers on the left side of the lowered finger is the tens of the answer, the number of fingers on the right side represents the ones. Example, 5 X 9: count on your fingers to five, starting with your left little finger. Five is your left thumb, so turn it down. There are four fingers to the left and five fingers to the right of the turned thumb, therefore 9 X 5 = 45.

If the student knows, or can figure, the 0's, 1's, 2's, 5's, and 9's, and the principle of commutativity (e.g., 3 X 5 = 5 X 3), it can be shown that there are only 15 facts left to learn. These facts are: 3 X 3, 3 X 4, 3 X 6, 3 X 7, 3 X 8; 4 X 4, 4 X 6, 4 X 7, 4 X 8; 6 X 6; 6 X 7; 6 X 8; 7 X 7, 7 X 8; 8 X 8.

Patricia Willott (1982) investigated the effects of pegword type elaborations on the retention of multiplication facts. She found that such techniques were very effective for learning selected multiplication facts of the type given above. However, she first had to develop pegwords for numbers above 10, and came up with the following:

Numeral	*Pegword(s)*
twenty	plenty (although Browning's "twin-ty" might be more effective)
thirty	dirty
forty	warty
fifty	gifty (i.e., gift-wrapped)
sixty	witchy
seventy	heavenly

So, for example, to teach 7 X 8 = 56, Willott showed a picture of heaven (represented as a cloud) with a gate (7 X 8), and next to the gate were *gifty sticks* (a bunch of sticks with a ribbon and bow around them). Now, using this system, see how many you can come up with. Our own selections are in the Appendix.

Fact	*Strategy*
3 X 3 = 9	
3 X 4 = 12	
3 X 6 = 18	

$$3 \times 7 = 21$$
$$3 \times 8 = 24$$
$$4 \times 4 = 16$$
$$4 \times 6 = 24$$
$$4 \times 7 = 28$$
$$4 \times 8 = 32$$
$$6 \times 6 = 36$$
$$6 \times 7 = 42$$
$$6 \times 8 = 48$$
$$7 \times 7 = 49$$
$$7 \times 8 = 56$$
$$8 \times 8 = 64$$

First Letter Strategies

Jeremy Kilpatrick, from the University of Georgia, has described two first letter strategies for learning operations (Kilpatrick, 1985). First, students can be taught "My Dear Aunt Sally" to remember the sequence of operations (Multiply and divide, add and subtract) in an expression without grouping symbols, such as $2 + 5 \times 6 - 1$.

Kilpatrick also described the use of the acronym FOIL to retrieve the sequence of operations in multiplying two binomials. The product $(a + b)(c + d)$ is the product of the first terms (ac), the outer terms (ad), the inner terms (bc), and the last terms (bd).

Yodai Mnemonics

A Japanese educator, Masachika Nakane, developed mnemonic systems for use with his Japanese students. He named these mnemonics "*Yodai*," meaning "the essence of structure," because they attempt to summarize the structures of problem solving into short essential phrases.

Unlike previously studied mnemonic systems which help improve memory for associations, Yodai mnemonics are intended to help students learn and recall the orderly cognitive processes required for problem solving. For this reason, Yodai mnemonics are sometimes called "process mnemonics."

To our knowledge, Yodai mnemonics have not been used with special or remedial students; in fact, most applications have been in Japanese schools. It is often difficult to translate this highly verbal procedure into meaningful English equivalents. Nevertheless, some of the techniques appear promising and are presented below. In English, they have been described by Higbee and Kunihira (1985).

Fractions. In Japan, children are taught to use bugs as visual images. In California, however, it was thought that swimming pools and joggers would be more familiar to children. These mnemonics are called POOL mnemonics, and some examples of these have been provided by Machida and Carlson (1984). The rhyme used is *"POOL* (or, put together) *shirts* (numerators) *to shirts, patches* (denominators) *to patches."* Students are shown a picture of a swimming pool in the shape of the multiplication symbol. A jogger, wearing shirt and shorts, is on each side. On each shirt is the numerator of a fraction, on the patches of the shorts, the denominator.

For addition and subtraction of fractions with equal denominators, the game is called *Match Patch,* and the rhyme is, *"Match the patch, don't take a chance. Count the shirts and leave the pants."* When fractions have unequal denominators, the rhyme is, *"If the patches do not match, POOL the other person's patch."*

Students are taught that *multi-POOL* stands for multiplication, and the rhyme is, *"POOL* (multiply together) *shirts to shirts, patches to patches."* For division (the *DIVE-ide* game), students are taught to invert the divisor and multiply. In that case, the rhyme taught is *"Flip* (invert) *the fool into the POOL"* (that is, multiply). The division sign is shown as a diving board with a beach ball on top and bottom.

Figure 7.5 "My Dear Aunt Sally" = Multiplication, Division, Addition, and Subtraction

Other operations. Multiplying binomials in the form (a + b) (c + d) is expressed as a wrestling tag team match, in which each wrestler of each team (east or west) wrestles with each member of the other team, thus (a + b) (c + d) = ac + ad + bc + bd.

Multiplying a mononomial by a polynomial in the form a (b + c + d) employs a Japanese folk tale about a boy (a) who is on a journey. On his way, he meets a dog (b), a pheasant (c), and a monkey (d) and takes each along with him. Therefore, a(b + c + d) = ab + ac + ad.

Yodai mnemonics have not been widely used in this country, partly because direct translation of the rhymes between Japanese into English has been difficult. However, there is accumulating evidence that Yodai mnemonics will someday prove very effective in teaching certain mathematics operations.

A MNEMONIC MATH LESSON

Review of Previous Information. Teacher: Last week, we finished covering some "5s" multiplication facts that you needed to learn. Let's review them today [Reviews facts].

Statement of Lesson Objective. Today, we are going to learn some difficult "6s" multiplication facts. To learn them, we're going to use the pegwords you have all learned earlier. Is everybody ready?

Presentation of New Information. The facts we're going to learn today are: 6 X 6, 6 X 7, and 6 X 8. Let's start with the first one.

Six times six is *thirty-six*. What is six times six, everybody? Good, Thirty-six. Janie, what is the pegword for six? Sticks, good. And Willy, what is the pegword for thirty? Good, dirty. So, Paula, what is the pegword for thirty-six? Dirty sticks, correct.

[shows picture] So, to remember six times six, remember: *Sticks, sticks,* and *dirty sticks.* You can remember this from the picture of someone washing piles of sticks. Two piles have been washed and one is still dirty. The man says, "Sticks, sticks, and dirty sticks." What does he say, class? [Class responds]. And what does sticks, sticks, and dirty sticks mean? [Class responds: "Six times six is thirty six"]. Good. So, what is six times six? Good.

Six times seven is *forty-two.* What is the pegword for six, Anna? And for seven, Fernando? Good. Here's a hard one for Sharon: What is the pegword for forty-two? Good, warty shoe.

[Shows picture]. To remember six times seven is forty-two, remember this picture. In the picture, *sticks* in *heaven* hold a *warty shoe.* What do sticks in heaven hold? And what is a warty shoe? Good, forty-two. Now, everybody say the whole thing together: "Sticks in heaven, warty shoe — Six times seven is forty-two." Good.

Here's the last one: Six times eight is forty-eight. What is the pegword for six, Billy? And eight, Maria? And forty-eight, Willy? Good, sticks, gate, and warty gate.

[Shows picture]. To remember six times eight is forty-eight, remember this picture of *sticks* on a *gate*, and a *warty gate*. What's next to sticks on a gate? Right, a warty gate. And what is a warty gate? Good, forty eight. Now, everybody say the whole thing together: "Sticks on a gate, warty gate — Six times eight is forty-eight." Good.

Guided Practice Now, everybody pay attention while we practice these three facts. I might call on you alone, or I might call on the whole class. [Practices facts with class].

Independent Practice Now I'm going to hand out some worksheets for you to practice independently. After you answer each problem, write the strategy we went over just now.

Evaluation Everybody take out a pencil and piece of paper, and I'll ask you to write the facts we studied today.

SUMMARY

This chapter has been concerned with the use of mnemonic techniques to improve students' command of basic skills, such as reading decoding, spelling, and math facts, procedures, and concepts. It has been emphasized that, although mnemonic instructional strategies will help students' initial acquisition of these skill areas, fluency in applying these skills will require additional guided and independent practice. Nevertheless, these mnemonic strategies may be just what some students need to get their basic skills off to a good start. In the next chapter we discuss a problem of major importance to teachers: how to help students generate these strategies independently.

CHAPTER 8

Teaching Students to Use These Strategies Independently

In the first chapter of this book, we referred to a commonly asked question: "Can students be taught to use these mnemonic strategies independently?" The answer to this question is a resounding Yes! Students can be taught to create mnemonic strategies independently (and to *generalize* their use). Students who learn to generate their own mnemonic pictures and images will be able to use these techniques for learning in other school situations, outside of school, and later in life (see also Pressley et al., 1991, Chaps.1 & 8).

The benefits of teaching students to generalize mnemonic strategy use are clear. However, it is important to remember that *students are unlikely to generalize mnemonic strategy use without explicit instruction for generalization.* Students have failed to independently generate even one mnemonic strategy, after as much as six weeks of intensive mnemonic instruction (Mastropieri & Scruggs, 1988). Many particularly difficult-to-teach students will not begin to develop their own strategies simply because they have previously been taught using mnemonics.

In some cases, explicit instructions to use mnemonic strategies can be helpful in promoting some generalized strategy use. True generalization training also requires very explicit procedures to develop students' understanding of where, when, and how to independently generate memory strategies. The important steps necessary for training students to generalize mnemonic strategies are presented in this chapter.

GENERALIZATION

Generalization refers to the use of specific behaviors or cognitive routines e.g., a mnemonic technique, outside the situations in which they were directly taught. A student who has learned a specific social skill in the classroom can be said to have generalized that skill if it is used appropriately in a situation outside the classroom. In many cases, generalization is the ultimate goal of skill-based classroom instruction.

Although there are a variety of cognitive strategies which are helpful in school learning situations, it is helpful to distinguish between those strategies that are *content-free* and those strategies that are *content-bound*. Content-free strategies are those that can be generally applied to a wide domain of content, while content-bound strategies are those that can be used for only one particular piece of information. For example, the "Cover-Copy-Compare" strategy for studying spelling words involves saying the word, covering it while copying, and finally, comparing the copied word with the original. This strategy can be used for studying any given list of spelling words, and is therefore content free.

An example: the mnemonic for remembering the vowels in the spelling word "cemetery": "She screamed E-E-E as she walked by the cEmEtEry" is used to learn the spelling of one word, while with the "Cover-Copy-Compare" strategy, it can be easily applied to all words.

Content-free and content-bound strategies should not be regarded as competing types of strategies; rather, they address different aspects of learning. For instance, it may be helpful to teach the spelling mnemonic (E-E-E) for remembering the spelling of the word cemetery; however, the "cover-copy-compare" strategy would be good for practicing the retrieval of this spelling mnemonic (along with that of other target words).

Content-free strategies are of little or no use if they do not generalize to task-appropriate situations. That is, it is of no use to learn cover-copy-compare, if this strategy is not used in actual learning situations.

Most of the mnemonic techniques discussed in this book are content-bound. A different reconstruction must be developed for each piece of information which needs to be remembered. A strategy to teach students to use mnemonics independently would in itself be a content-free strategy, and students could then use this overall strategy for developing mnemonics to a wide variety of content domains. The next section discusses a content-free strategy for promoting independent mnemonic strategy development.

How Strategies Generalize

Generalization of cognitive strategies requires practice, insight, and effort. In our book, *Effective Instruction for Special Education*, we describe the specific steps for independently executing any cognitive routine:

1. The student must *recognize that the strategy is called for*. This ability has been called by some *meta-cognition* or *executive functioning*, and refers to a student's awareness of the learning process and

how it relates to specific instances. For example, the student, when confronted with a list of spelling words, should realize that a specific strategy (e.g., cover-copy-compare) is called for.

2. The student must *remember and use the specific steps in the strategy*. In the spelling example, the student must remember all steps in the process of executing the strategy, including a preliminary reading of the list, covering the list, copying the spelling words, and comparing the list with the student's spellings. After self-administered feedback to see how many were correct, the process is repeated until all words have been spelled correctly.

3. The student must *correctly execute the strategy*. It is possible to retrieve the individual steps in a cognitive routine without executing these steps correctly. It should be noted that executing the strategy correctly is a separate step from remembering the steps in the strategy. Efficient strategy execution is something that must be practiced frequently until mastered.

Attribution. Research has shown that students are more likely to use effective cognitive strategies when they come to *attribute* their learning success to the use of these strategies. It is important that teachers reinforce the effectiveness of using the strategy to learn specific materials in their teaching. If students fail to learn, teachers should help the student see that he or she failed to execute the appropriate cognitive strategy correctly, rather than attributing the failure to a general lack of effort, or worse yet, general overall characterizations, such as "stupid" or "lazy". Students can understand what to do differently the next time they try when you stress the elements in correct strategy use. When students are successful at learning, teachers must help them see that it was due to the student's diligence in applying the appropriate cognitive strategy(ies). Such statements as, "Yes! You answered that correctly because you used the strategy we talked about!" or, "The reason you didn't learn this information is that you didn't apply the strategy we practiced in class," can be very effective in helping students attribute their learning to their use of strategies.

Attribution training, especially with students who have a history of learning failure, helps students to move beyond ability explanations for learning failure toward more positive conceptualizations of themselves (Clifford, 1984). If a student believes he or she fails because he or she is "stupid," "dumb," or "lazy," the situation appears hopeless because these attributions seem permanent and unlikely to change. Likewise, attributing success to luck does little to encourage further efforts. But if a student attributes learning failure to a lack of strategy execution, this is something the student can work on. In discussing reasons for academic failure, it is always more productive to speak in terms of what a student *does* than to speak in terms of what a student *is* (or is not).

Research has indicated that many students with a history of learning failure display inappropriate attributions. They are likely to attribute their failures to their own lack of ability, and their successes to luck, difficulty level of the task ("it was easy"), or external support ("the teacher helped me"). Such thinking promotes low self-esteem in the student, now stirring a sense they cannot learn. To break this cycle of learning failure, students must be (1) provided with effective learning strategies, (2) taught to attribute their new success to these strategies, and (3) taught to apply the new strategies independently. The next section describes how you can promote independent use of mnemonic strategies.

PROMOTING TRANSFER OF MNEMONIC STRATEGIES

By now, you may have gotten the impression that creating effective mnemonic strategies can sometimes be difficult and time-consuming, especially as compared with much simpler (and much less effective) strategies such as rehearsal or simply memorizing. If this is true for teachers, it is even more true for students, and especially those in special education or remedial classes. Nevertheless, students can learn to develop their own mnemonics. Here are some suggestions for promoting independent strategy use:

1. *Incorporate mnemonic instruction as much as possible in your teaching.* Students are taught "theories of learning," as well as content, by their teachers. The teacher's style of teaching communicates not only content but also information about how people learn. For instance, if students are taught mainly by drill-and-practice and rehearsal, they begin to think that this is the best way to learn. If they are taught mainly by independent practice and worksheets, they will begin to think that this is the best way to learn. On the other hand, if students are taught using mnemonic strategies, they will begin to learn that such strategies can play an important role in learning. With a good deal of exposure to a variety of mnemonic strategies over time (hopefully, years), students see the value of these strategies in promoting efficient learning. However, exposure alone to mnemonic strategies will not guarantee that students will employ them independently.

2. *Effectively apply attributions.* Attributing success in learning and remembering to the use of appropriate mnemonic strategies enforces the relationship between these strategies and success.

3. *Prompt the systematic creation of mnemonic strategies.* Before students are provided with specific mnemonic strategies, the teacher could solicit ideas: "So, class, what we need to remember is that

Kansas is a major *wheat* producing state. What kind of picture do you think I need to help you remember that?" This will help students begin to think mnemonically. Feedback that you give, in the form of the picture, will help them compare their strategy with yours.

4. *Have the class create or apply the strategies.* Tell your class that, this week, you do not have any mnemonic pictures, and that you need to have them create the strategies. Select the important information, and ask students to "brainstorm" possible strategies. Remember to provide use of the rules for mnemonic strategy construction:

   a. Students should first *identify* the information to be connected or associated.

   b. They should then *reconstruct* the information into a more meaningful form. Using the principles of reconstructive elaborations, this means using acoustic, symbolic, or mimetic reconstructions, depending on whether information is unfamiliar, familiar but abstract, or familiar and concrete, respectively.

   c. Next, they should *relate* the reconstructed term to its associated information.

   d. Finally, they should correctly execute the steps necessary to *retrieve* the information when needed.

   When students have agreed on an optimal strategy, have students draw the picture for themselves. The artistic quality of the picture is not particularly important, as long as the picture is recognizable. Students who have drawn mnemonic pictures are more likely to have created an effective mental image.

5. Have each student independently *develop his or her own mnemonic strategies.* The teacher provides the information, and asks students to create their own choice. They should be told to brainstorm possibilities, choose the best alternative, and create a mnemonic picture. Students can compare their choices during or after class, and discuss them.

6. A final step is to *monitor and evaluate the creation of effective mnemonic strategies in other classrooms.* Students should be given feedback on choosing which information is most important (a task based as much on the values of the particular teacher as on an objective evaluation of text). Given that important information has been selected, students can be given feedback on the strategies they have chosen.

Some students may have great difficulty creating useful mnemonic pictures or images. These students should be encouraged to think of any way they can to make information more meaningful. Research has shown if students actively think about the information being taught, what it sounds like or otherwise reminds the students of, they will be more likely to retrieve the information than if they simply rehearse it.

FINAL CONSIDERATIONS

In teaching transfer of mnemonic strategies, it is important to remember that different objectives are being served than when information is being taught mnemonically. When teaching mnemonically, it is the *learning of the content* that is of most importance. When teaching for mnemonic transfer, it is the learning of *mnemonic strategy use* that is of most importance. This is important because our own research and experience has shown us that many students, particularly special or remedial students, often learn less information using their own mnemonic strategies than they will using the effective mnemonic strategies teachers have constructed and provided. Also, if mnemonic techniques have already been developed, students will not need to spend the time and effort developing mnemonic strategies.

Although it is important for students to develop methods for independent learning, it is also important for them to learn important school content. When strategies have already been created and are available, it is both prudent and efficient to use them. On the other hand, when students have a need to apply their own learning methods more effectively, especially when materials do not exist, it is important that they be taught skills for doing this. However students create mnemonic strategies, they are likely to learn more than if they did not create such strategies. It is known, for instance, that students who are known for having good memories frequently report using methods similar to these (Scruggs & Mastropieri, 1984, 1985), so it makes sense to help all students have the advantage of mnemonic strategies at their disposal. It is also true that teacher-developed mnemonic materials can be enormously effective in promoting school learning (Scruggs & Mastropieri, 1990). However it is used, mnemonic strategy instruction can become a very important asset for effective classroom teaching and student learning.

Bibliography

General Books That Present Mnemonic Techniques

Browning, W.G. (1983). *Memory power for exams*. Lincoln, Nebraska: Cliff Notes Inc. Provides information on a variety of study strategies.

Bullock, J., Pierce, S., & McClellan, L. (1987). *Touch math: Teacher's manual*. Colorado Springs, CO: Touch Learning Concepts. Describes applications of the Touch Math system.

Higbee, K.L. (1977). *Your memory, how it works, and how to improve it*. Englewood Cliffs, NJ: Prentice Hall. Provides a readable overview on human memory.

Hirsch, E.D., Jr. (1987). *Cultural literacy: What every American needs to know*. New York: Vintage Books. Describes the "Knowledge Crisis" in American schools and offers a list of core school information.

Lorayne, H. (19885). *Page a minute memory book*. New York: Holt, Rinehart, & Winston. Briefly describes popular memory techniques.

Lorayne, H., & Lucas, J. (1974). *The memory book*. New York: Ballantine Books. Provides a detailed description of memory strategies for personal use.

Shefter, H. (1976). *Six minutes a day to perfect spelling*. New York: Pocket Books. Describes many techniques for improving spelling, including the "spelling mnemonic" presented in this book.

Yates, F.A. (1966). *The art of memory*. Chicago: The University of Chicago Press. Provides an in-depth, academic discussion of the history of mnemonic techniques.

References

Atkinson, R.C. (1975). Mnemotechnics in second-language learning. *American Psychologist, 30*, 821-828.

Clifford, M.M. (1984). Thoughts on a theory of constructive failure. *Educational Psychologist, 19*, 108-120.

Ehri, L.C., Deffner, N.D., & Wilce, L.S. (1984). Pictorial mnemonics for phonics. *Journal of Educational Psychology, 76*, 880-893.

Herrmann, D.J., & Chaffin, R. (1988). *Memory in historical perspective: The literature before Ebbinghaus.* New York: Springer-Verlag.

Higbee, K.L., & Kunihira, S. (1985). Cross-cultural applications of Yodai mnemonics in education. *Educational Psychologist, 20,* 57-64.

Kilpatrick, J. (1985). Doing mathematics without understanding it: A commentary on Higbee and Kunihira. *Educational Psychologist, 20* (2), 65-68.

Levin, J. R., Dretzke, B. J., McCormick, C. B., Scruggs, T. E., McGivern, J. E., & Mastropieri, M. A. (1983). Learning via mnemonic pictures; Analysis of the presidential process. *Educational Communication and Technology Journal, 3,* 547-550.

Levin, J. R., Morrison, C. R., McGivern, J. E., Mastropieri, M. A., & Scruggs, T. E. (1986). Mnemonic facilitation of text-embedded science facts. *American Educational Research Journal, 23,* 489-506.

Luria, A. R. (1968). *The mind of mnemonist.* Cambridge, MA: Harvard University Press.

Machida, K., & Carlson, J. (1984). The effects of a verbal mediation strategy on cognitive processes in mathematics learning. *Journal of Educational Psychology, 76,* 1382-1385.

Mastropieri, M. A. (1988). Using the keyword method. *Teaching Exceptional Children, 20*(2), 4-8.

Mastropieri, M.A., Emerick, K., & Scruggs, T.E. (1988). Mnemonic instruction of science concepts. *Behavioral Disorders, 14,* 48-56.

Mastropieri, M.A., & Fulk, B.J.M. (1990). Optimizing academic performance with mnemonic instruction. In T.E. Scruggs & B.Y.L. Wong (Eds.), *Intervention research in learning disabilities*. New York: Springer-Verlag.

Mastropieri, M. A., & Scruggs, T. E. (1984). Generalization of academic and social behaviors: Five effective strategies. *Academic Therapy, 19*, 427-432.

Mastropieri, M. A., & Scruggs, T. E. (1987). *Effective instruction for special education*. Boston: Little, Brown/College Hill.

Mastropieri, M.A. & Scruggs, T.E. (1988). Increasing the content area learning of learning disabled students: Research implementation. *Learning Disabilities Research, 4*, 17-25.

Mastropieri, M.A., & Scruggs, T.E. (1989). Reconstructive elaborations: Strategies that facilitate content learning. *Learning Disabilities Focus, 4*, 73-77.

Mastropieri, M. A., & Scruggs, T. E. (1989). Mnemonic social studies instruction: Classroom applications. *Remedial and Special Education, 10*(3), 40-46.

Mastropieri, M. A., & Scruggs, T. E. (1989). Constructing more meaningful relationships: Mnemonic instruction for special populations. *Educational Psychology Review, 1*, 83-111.

Mastropieri, M.A., & Scruggs, T.E. (1989). Reconstructive elaborations: Strategies for adapting content area information. *Academic Therapy, 24*, 391-406.

Mastropieri, M.A., Scruggs, T.E., & Fulk, B.J.M. (1990). Teaching abstract vocabulary with the keyword method: Effects on recall and comprehension. *Journal of Learning Disabilities, 23*, 92-96.

Mastropieri, M. A., Scruggs, T. E., & Levin, J. R. (1983). Pictorial mnemonic strategies for special education. *Journal of Special Education Technology, 6*, 24-33.

Mastropieri, M. A., Scruggs, T. E., & Levin, J. R. (1984). Research in progress: Mnemonic strategies for handicapped and gifted learners. *Exceptional Children, 50*, 559.

Mastropieri, M. A., Scruggs, T. E. & Levin, J. R. (1985). Maximizing what exceptional students can learn: A review of research on the keyword method and related mnemonic techniques. *Remedial and Special Education, 6*(2), 39-45.

Mastropieri, M. A., Scruggs, T. E., & Levin, J. R. (1985). Mnemonic strategy instruction with learning disabled adolescents. *Journal of Learning Disabilities, 18*, 94-100.

Mastropieri, M. A., Scruggs, T. E., & Levin, J. R. (1986). Direct vs. mnemonic instruction: Relative benefits for exceptional learners. *Journal of Special Education, 20*, 299-308.

Mastropieri, M. A., Scruggs, T. E., & Levin, J. R. (1987). Increasing LD students' recall of facts from expository prose. *American Educational Research Journal, 24*, 505-519.

Mastropieri, M. A., Scruggs, T. E., & Levin, J. R. (1987). Mnemonic strategies in special education. In M. McDaniel & M. Pressley (Eds.), *Imaginal and mnemonic processes* (pp 358-376). New York: Springer-Verlag.

Mastropieri, M. A., Scruggs, T. E., & Levin, J. R., Gaffney, J., & McLoone, B. (1985) Mnemonic vocabulary instruction for learning disabled students. *Learning Disability Quarterly, 8*, 57-63.

Mastropieri, M. A., Scruggs, T. E., & Levin, J. R., McLoone, B. (1985). Facilitating learning disabled students acquisition of science classifications. *Learning Disability Quarterly, 8*, 299-309.

McDaniel, M.A., & Pressley, M. (1989). Keyword and context instruction of new vocabulary meanings: Effects on text comprehension and memory. *Journal of Educational Psychology, 81*, 204-213.

McLoone, B. B., Scruggs, T. E., Mastropieri, M. A., & Zucker, S. (1986). Memory strategy instruction and training with LD adolescents. *Learning Disabilities Research, 2*, 45-53.

Pressley, M., & Associates. (1990). *Cognitive strategy instruction that really improves children's academic performance.* Cambridge, MA: Brookline.

Pressley, M., Borkowski, J.G., & Schneider, W. (1987). Cognitive strategies: Good strategy users coordinate metacognition and knowledge. *Annals of Child Development, 4*, 89-129.

Pressley, M., & Levin, J.R. (Eds.) (1983). *Cognitive strategy training: Educational applications and theoretical foundations.* New York: Springer-Verlag.

Pressley, M., Levin, J.R., & Delaney, H.D. (1982). The mnemonic keyword method. *Review of Educational Research, 52*, 61-91.

Pressley, M., Levin, J.R., & McDaniel, M.A. (1987). Remembering versus inferring what a word means: Mnemonic and contextual approaches. In M.G. McKeown & M.E. Curtis (Eds.), *The nature of vocabulary instruction* (pp. 107-127). Hillsdale, NJ: Erlbaum.

Pressley, M., Levin, J.R., & Miller, G.E. (1981). How does the keyword method affect vocabulary comprehension and usage? *Reading Research Quarterly, 16*, 213-226.

Pressley, M., Samuel, J., Hershey, M.M., Bishop, S.L., & Dickinson, D. (1981). Use of a mnemonic technique to teach young children foreign language vocabulary. *Contemporary Educational Psychology, 6*, 110-116.

Pressley, M., Scruggs, T. E., & Mastropieri, M. A. (1989). Memory strategy instruction for learning disabilities: Present and future directions for researchers. *Learning Disabilities Research, 4*, 68-77.

Pressley, M., Symons, S.E., Snyder, B.L., & Cariglia-Bull, T. (1989). Strategy instruction research is coming of age. *Learning Disability Quarterly, 12*, 16-30.

Scruggs, T.E., & Laufenberg, R. (1986). Transformational mnemonic strategies for retarded learners. *Education and Training of the Mentally Retarded, 21*, 65-73.

Scruggs, T. E., & Mastropieri, M. A. (1984). How gifted students learn: Implications from recent research. *Roeper Review, 6*, 183-185.

Scruggs, T.E., & Mastropieri, M.A. (1984). Improving memory for facts: The "keyword" method. *Academic Therapy, 20*, 159-166.

Scruggs, T. E., & Mastropieri, M. A. (1984). Issues in generalization: Implications for special education. *Psychology in the Schools, 21*, 397-403.

Scruggs, T. E., & Mastropieri, M. A. (1985). Spontaneous verbal elaboration in gifted and non-gifted youths. *Journal for the Education of the Gifted, 9*, 1-10.

Scruggs, T. E., & Mastropieri, M. A. (1987). Keyword method. In C. Reynolds & L. Mann (Eds.), *Encyclopedia of special education: A reference for the education of the handicapped and other exceptional children and adults* (vol. 11, p. 894-895). New York: Wiley.

Scruggs, T. E., & Mastropieri, M. A. (1988). Acquisition and transfer of mnemonic strategies by gifted and non-gifted students.

Journal of Special Education, 22, 153-166.

Scruggs, T.E., & Mastropieri, M.A. (1989). Mnemonic instruction of learning disabled students: A field-based evaluation. *Learning Disability Quarterly, 12,* 119-125.

Scruggs, T.E., & Mastropieri, M.A. (1989). Reconstructive elaborations: A model for content area learning. *American Educational Research Journal, 26,* 311-327.

Scruggs, T.E., & Mastropieri, M.A. (1990). The case for mnemonic instruction: From laboratory investigations to classroom applications. *Journal of Special Education,*

Scruggs, T.E., & Mastropieri, M.A. (in press). Mnemonic classroom instruction: Acquisition, maintenance, and generalization. *Exceptional Children.*

Scruggs, T. E., Mastropieri, M. A., Jorgensen, C., & Monson, J. A. (1986). Effective mnemonic strategies for gifted learners. *Journal for the Education of the Gifted, 9,* 105-121.

Scruggs, T. E., Mastropieri, M. A., & Levin, J. R. (1985). Vocabulary acquisition by mentally retarded students under direct and mnemonic instruction. *American Journal of Mental Deficiency, 89,* 546-551.

Scruggs, T. E., Mastropieri, M. A., & Levin, J. R. (1986). Can children effectively re-use the same mnemonic pegwords? *Educational Communication and Technology Journal, 34,* 83-88.

Scruggs, T. E., Mastropieri, M. A., & Levin, J. R. (1987). Implications of mnemonic strategy research for theories of learning disabilities. In H. L. Swanson (Ed.), *Memory and learning disabilities: Advances in learning and behavior disabilities* (pp. 225-244). Greenwich, CT: JAI Press.

Scruggs, T. E., Mastropieri, M. A., Levin, J. R., & Gaffney, J. S. (1985). Facilitating the acquisition of science facts in learning disabled students. *American Educational Research Journal, 22,* 575-586.

Scruggs, T. E., Mastropieri, M. A., Levin, J. R., McLoone, B. B., Gaffney, J. S., & Prater, M. (1985). Increasing content area learning: A comparison of mnemonic and visual-spatial direct instruction. *Learning Disabilities Research, 1,* 18-31.

Scruggs, T. E., Mastropieri, M. A., McLoone, B. B., Levin, J. R. & Morrison, C. (1987). Mnemonic facilitation of text-embedded science facts with LD students. *Journal of Educational Psychology,* *79,* 27-34.

Scruggs, T. E., Mastropieri, M. A., Monson, J. A., & Jorgensen, C. (1985). Maximizing what gifted students can learn: Recent findings of learning strategy research. *Gifted Child Quarterly, 29,* 181-185.

Seamon, J. G. (1980). *Human memory.* New York: Oxford University Press.

Sheikh, A. A., & Sheikh, K. S. (1985). *Imagery in education.* Farmingdale, NY: Baywood Publishing.

Taylor, S.C. (1981). *The keyword mnemonic method for teaching vocabulary: Its use by learning disabled children with memory problems.* Unpublished doctoral dissertation, Oklahoma State University, Stillwater.

Veit, D., Scruggs, T. E., & Mastropieri, M. A. (1986). Extended mnemonic instruction with learning disabled students. *Journal of Educational Psychology, 78,* 300-308.

Willott, P.C. (1982). *The use of imagery as a mnemonic to teach basic multiplication facts to students with learning disabilities.* Unpublished doctoral dissertation, West Virginia University, Morgantown.

Appendix

Answers to Chapter 2 Exercises

Abstract Vocabulary Words

1. Vituperation (viper): A viper speaking abusively to someone.

2. Objurgation (jury): A jury giving a person a vehement chiding.

3. Nonage (nun): A Nun telling two kids they are too young to get married.

4. Saprophytic (Sapro the fighting tick): Sapro the fighting tick is sitting on and eating decaying matter.

5. Nepenthe (Neptune): The god Neptune is dispensing drugs to people to help them decrease feelings of sorrow.

6. Octroi (octopus): An octopus is at a toll booth collecting taxes from people who have certain goods entering a town.

7. Amerce (hammer): A police officer is hammering on a person's car and saying: I punish you by imposing a fine.

8. Bewray (bees): Two bees talking and betraying secrets.

9. Buncombe (buns): A boring speech is being given and participants are throwing buns at the speaker saying: This is boring!

10. Intercalate (percolate): A coffee percolator is spitting on extra days to the calendar.

Word Parts

1. Bronto (bronco) A bronco bucking in the thunder.

2. Paleo (old) Old people carrying pails.

3. Sauro (sawing) A lizard sawing

4. Thero (thermos) A wild animal having a drink from a thermos.

5. Ornith (oar) A bird carrying an oar.

6. Ptero (tire) A tire with wings.

7. Poda (pod) A foot kicking a pod.

Italian Words

	Italian Word	Keyword	Interactive Sentence
1.	Roccia	(roach)	A roach jumping off a cliff.
2.	Mela	(mail)	An apple in a mailbox.
3.	Coniglio	(cone)	A rabbit with an ice cream cone.
4.	Coltre	(colt)	A colt with a blanket on it.
5.	Capre	(cop)	A goat dressed up as a cop.
6.	Lago	(log)	Lots of logs floating in a lake.
7.	Carta	(cart)	A cart filled with paper.
8.	Barca	(bark)	A barking dog sitting in a boat.
9.	Fonda	(phone)	A phone in a bag.
10.	Strada	(straw)	A road covered with straw.

Answers to Chapter 3 Exercises

Minerals

Keywords and interactive pictures for mineral hardness levels follow below:

Name	Keyword	Hardness	Pegword	Picture
Bauxite	Box	1	Bun	A *box* of *buns*
Gypsum	Gypsy	2	Shoe	A *Gypsy* in dancing *shoes*.
Calcite	Cow	3	Tree	A *cow* in a *tree*.
Rhodochrosite	Road	4	Door	A *road* going through a *door*.
Apatite	Ape	5	Hive	An *ape* poking a *hive*.
Feldspar	Field	6	Sticks	A *field* of *sticks*.
Starolite	Star	7	Heaven	A *star* in *heaven*.
Beryl	Barrel	8	Gate	A *barrel* at a *gate*.

The Planets

Following are the mnemonic strategies for learning the order of the planets of the solar system:

Planet	Keyword	Order	Pegword	Picture
Mercury	Mermaid	1	Bun	A *mermaid* eating *buns*.
Venus	Venus	2	shoe	A statue of *Venus* wearing *shoes*.
Earth	Ear	3	tree	An *ear* in a *tree*.
Mars	Martian	4	four	A *Martian* (alien with antennas) opening a *door*
Jupiter	Soup	5	five	Bees in a *hive* eating *soup*.
Saturn	Sat on	6	sticks	Someone *sat on* a pile of *sticks*.
Uranus	Rain	7	heaven	A *rain* storm in *heaven*.
Neptune	Neptune	8	gate	The god *Neptune* opening a *gate*.
Pluto	Glue	9	vine	*Vines* stuck together with *glue*.

All of the above should be pictured with a solar system in the background to help retrieve the meaning of the list.

Figure A.l Mercury (mermaid) = Planet #1 (bun)

Answers to Chapter 5 Social Studies Exercises

Transportation

Stimulus	Reconstruction	Interactive Elaboration
Transportation	train	train filled with cars, boats, trucks, and other means of transportation
Trace	race	early pioneers having a race down a trace, or narrow trail
Corduroy Road	cord	pioneers wrapping cords around logs and placing them in muddy places in the road
Plank Road	plant	plants growing all around the flat split logs on the road
Cumberland Road National Road	cucumber Uncle Sam	Uncle Sam standing on a gravel road collecting dollars and saying: "Thank you for your tax dollars in building the National Road." Someone else is selling cucumbers and a sign says: "Cucumbers for sale. Eat Cucumbers on the Cumberland Road. There is also a big bag of gravel on the gravel road, and a sign saying the National Road connects the East and the West.
Interstate	interstate highway	Picture two people Highway driving on a highway. They are leaving one state (Indiana) and entering another state (Illinois). The driver is saying to the passenger: "This highway *goes between different states.*" The passenger responds by saying: "Yes, It's an *inter-state highway.*"

Indiana's Natural Resources

1. Indiana has good soil in the north and poor soil in the south. All the information is considered to be familiar to our students, because they are from Indiana. Therefore, mimetic reconstructions are necessary for learning the information. *Mimetic reconstruction:* A picture of a map of Indiana, that contains a farmer in the northern part of the state with his good, healthy crops, because of the good soil, and a farmer in the southern part of the state next to his small unhealthy crops, because the soil is poor. If your own students were not familiar with Indiana, you might need an acoustic reconstruction for Indiana, "Indian", and then have the Indian standing with the crops, rather than the farmer.

2. Nearly 3/4 of the state of Indiana is cultivated. This means crops are planted on it. Cultivate is considered to be unfamiliar and nonmeaningful for our students; therefore, an acoustic reconstruction is needed for the word cultivate, and the definition of cultivate can be mimetically reconstructed. "Colt" is a good acoustic reconstruction because it sounds like the first syllable of cultivate, it is familiar to our students, and it is easily pictured. Then a good elaboration is a picture of a "colt" taking care of the land so crops can be grown. The colt is cultivating the land.

3. Corn is the number one crop in Indiana. All of this information is familiar to our students because they are from Indiana. Mimetic reconstructions and a good elaboration consists of a map of Indiana with a big corn stalk in the middle of the state with the statement: "Corn is Number One in Indiana." Again, the Indian could be holding the corn stalk and saying: Corn is Number one in Indiana, for those unfamiliar with Indiana.

4. Soybeans are also an important crop in Indiana. Soybeans have many uses including: baby food, feed for animals, and making soap and candles. The terms soybeans, baby food, animal food, and soap and candles are all familiar and meaningful to our students. Therefore, mimetic reconstructions are necessary for all, and a good interactive elaboration must have all the components to be remembered interacting. In this case a picture of a big bag of soybeans being poured into a baby food jar, while the baby is feeding her pet with soybean food, and a mama is washing the baby's face with soybean soap, to remove the excess soybean food from the baby's face. If soybean were an unfamiliar term, the term bean might be used to illustrate that soybeans are a particular type of bean, and then this picture could be seen interacting with the products made from soybeans. And, the Indian could be

shown pouring the bag of beans to assist with the connection that soybeans are from Indiana.

5. Crop rotation means planting the same crops in a different place each year to help the soil. Rotation was a completely unfamiliar word for our students; therefore, an acoustic reconstruction was necessary. "Row" is considered to be a good acoustic reconstruction because it sounds like rotation, is familiar to the students, and is easily pictured. A good interactive elaboration might be a picture of a farmer saying: "We rotate these crops in rows. This means we plant different crops in the same place each year." The picture could contain various rows of different crops with signs saying : Corn Year 1; Soybeans Year 2.

States and Capitals

1. The keyword for Alabama is *band*. The keyword for the capital, Montgomery, is *monkey*. Think of a picture of monkeys playing in a band.

2. The keywords for Alaska are *"I'll ask her"*. The keywords for the capital, Juneau are *"Do you know?"*. Think of a picture of a boy asking another boy *"Do you know* the capital of Alaska?" He replies by pointing to a girl and saying *"I'll ask her."*

3. The keywords for Arizona are *arid zone*. The keywords for the capital, Phoenix are *PHONE X*. Think of a picture of PHONE X in an arid zone.

4. The keyword for Arkansas is *ark*. The keywords for Little Rock are little rock. Think of a picture of an ark bumping into a little rock.

5. The keywords for California are *calf's horn*. The keywords for the capital, Sacramento, is *sack of mint*. Think of a picture of a sack of mint on a calf's horn.

6. The keyword for Colorado is *coloring*. The keyword for the capital, Denver, is *den*. Think of a picture of children coloring at the coloring den.

7. The keyword for Connecticut is *convict*. The keyword for the capital, Hartford, is *heart*. Think of a picture of a convict breaking heart-shaped rocks.

8. The keyword for Delaware is *devil*. The keyword for the capital, Dover, is *dove*. Think of a picture of a devil holding a dove.

9. The keyword for Florida is *flower*. The keyword for the capital, Tallahassee, is *television*. Think of a picture of a flower on top of a television.

10. The keywords for Georgia are *George Washington*. The keywords for the capital, Atlanta, are *Atlantic Ocean*. Think of a picture of George Washington standing in the Atlantic Ocean.

11. The keywords for Hawaii are *"How are ya?"*. The keywords for the capital, Honolulu, are *Honey, I'm Lou*. Think of a picture of a Hawaiian woman asking ,"How are ya?" and he says,"Honey I'm Lou."

12. The keywords for Idaho are *"I don't know"*. The keyword for the capital, Boise, is *boys*. Think of a picture of boys saying "I don't know" when the teacher asks them "What is the answer, boys?".

13. The keyword for Illinois is *ill*. The keyword for the capital, Springfield, is *spring*. Think of a picture of a man who drank from the spring and is feeling ill.

14. The keyword for Indiana is *Indian*. The keywords for the capital, Indianapolis, are *Indianapolis 500*. Think of a picture of an Indian driving a race car in the Indianapolis 500.

15. The keywords for Iowa are *I owe ya*. The keywords for the capital, Des Moines, are *de mines*. Think of a picture of a boss of de mines telling a person "I owe ya" his paycheck.

16. The keyword for Kansas is *can*. The keyword for the capital, Topeka, is *top*. Think of a picture of a top spinning on top of a can.

17. The keyword for Kentucky is *kennel*. The keyword for the capital, Frankfort, is *frankfurters*. Think of a picture of dogs in a kennel eating frankfurters.

18. The keywords for Louisiana are *Louise & Anna*. The keywords for the capital, Baton Rouge, are *baton & rouge*. Think of a picture of girls twirling batons and wearing rouge on their cheeks.

19. The keywords for Maine are *horse's mane*. The keywords for the capital, Augusta, are *gust of wind*. Think of a picture of a horse's mane being blown by a gust of wind.

20. The keyword for Maryland is *marry*. The keyword for the capital, Annapolis, is *apple*. Think of a picture of a married couple eating an apple.

21. The keyword for Massachusetts is *mast*. The keyword for the capital, Boston, is *boxer*. Think of a picture of a boxer trying to fight someone hiding behind the mast of a ship.

22. The keywords for Michigan are *pitch again*. The keyword for the capital, Lansing, is *lamb*. Think of a picture of a lamb at bat telling the pitcher to pitch again.

23. The keywords for Minnesota are *mini-soda*. The keywords for the capital, St. Paul, are, *St. Paul*. Think of a picture of an angel named St. Paul with a mini-soda.

24. The keyword for Mississippi is *misses*. The keyword for the capital, Jackson, is *jacks*. Think of a picture of two girls (misses) playing with jacks.

25. The keyword for Missouri is *misery*. The keyword for the capital, Jefferson City, is *chef*. Think of a picture of a chef who is in misery because his cake fell.

26. The keyword for Montana is *mountain*. The keyword for the capital, Helena, is *Helen*. Think of a picture of a woman named Helen at the top of a mountain.

27. The keywords for Nebraska are *new brass*. The keywords for the capital, Lincoln, are *Abe Lincoln*. Think of a picture of Abe Lincoln shining his new brass pot.

28. The keywords for Nevada are *new ladder*. The keywords for the capital, Carson City, are *Car City*. Think of a picture of a man climbing a new ladder to get to Car City.

29. The keyword for New Hampshire is *hamster*. The keyword for the capital, Concord, is *Concorde*. Think of a picture of a hamster flying a Concorde jet.

30. The keyword for New Jersey is *jersey*. The keyword for the capital, Trenton, is *tent*. Think of a picture of a tent with a jersey on it.

31. The keyword for New Mexico is *Mexico*. The keywords for the capital, Santa Fe, are *Santa Claus*. Think of a picture of Santa Claus going into Mexico.

32. The keywords for New York are *new pork*. The keywords for the capital, Albany, are *all baloney*. Think of a picture of a woman asking the butcher if the meat is new pork and the butcher responds by saying: "It's all baloney!"

33. The keyword for North Carolina is *carolers*. The keyword for the capital, Raleigh, is *trolley*. Think of a picture of carolers riding a trolley going north.

34. The keywords for North Dakota are *northern coat*. The keywords for the capital, Bismarck, are *business man*. Think of a picture of a business man wearing a coat for cold, northern weather.

35. The keywords for Ohio are *oh, Hi*. The keywords for the capital, Columbus, are *Christopher Columbus*. Think of a picture of a person saying, "Oh, hi Columbus."

36. The keywords for Oklahoma are *oak home*. The keywords for the capital, Oklahoma City, are *oak home city*. Think of a picture of builder telling someone he's building an oak home in Oak Home City.

37. The keyword for Oregon is *ore*. The keyword for the capital, Salem, is *sailboat*. Think of a picture of a sailboat with a load of ore.

38. The keyword for Pennsylvania is *pen*. The keyword for the capital, Harrisburg, is *hairy*. Think of a picture of a hairy pen.

39. The keywords for Rhode Island are *road to an island*. The keywords for the capital, Providence, are *prove it*. Think of a picture one man on a road telling the other man that the road goes to an island. The other man says, "Prove it."

40. The keyword for South Carolina is *carolers*. The keywords for the capital, Columbia, is *column*. Think of a picture of carolers singing in front of a southern mansion with columns.

41. The keywords for South Dakota are *southern coat*. The keyword for the capital, Pierre, is *pier*. Think of a picture of a man standing on a pier wearing a coat for warm, southern weather.

42. The keyword for Tennessee is *tennis*. The keyword for the capital, Nashville, is *cash*. Think of a picture of people paying cash to play tennis.

43. The keyword for Texas is *taxes*. The keyword for Austin, is *ostrich*. Think of a picture of an ostrich paying taxes.

44. The keywords for Utah are *you paws*. The keywords for the capital, Salt Lake City, are *salt lake*. Think of a picture of a paws pouring salt into a lake, and a person yelling, "Hey you paws, stop that."

45. The keywords for Vermont is *worm mountain*. The keywords for the capital, Montpelier, are *mountain pliers*. Think of a picture of a mountain pliers taking a worm off the mountain.

46. The keyword for Virginia is *fur*. The keywords for the capital, Richmond, are *rich man*. Think of a picture of a rich man buying fur coats.

47. The keywords for Washington are *ton of wash*. The keyword for the capital, Olympia, is *olympic*. Think of a picture of people in an olympic event to do a ton of wash.

48. The keywords for West Virginia are *vest fur*. The keyword for the capital, Charleston, is *charcoal*. Think of a picture of a man lighting charcoal while wearing a vest made of fur.

49. The keywords for Wisconsin are *whisk broom*. The keyword for the capital, Madison, is *maid*. Think of a picture of a maid using a whisk broom to clean.

50. The keywords for Wyoming are *Y home*. The keywords for the capital, Cheyenne, are *shy Anne*. Think of a picture of a shy girl named Anne who lives in a Y-shaped home.

U.S. Presidents

President   *Strategy*

1. George Washington: *Washing* (Washington) *buns* (1) in a *spring garden* (first decade, 1-10 = 1).

2. John Adams: *Adding* (Adams) *shoes* (2) in a *spring garden* (1-10 = 2).

3. Thomas Jefferson: A *chef* (Jefferson) in a *tree* (3) in a *spring garden* (1-10 = 3).

4. James Madison: A *maid* (Madison) sweeping a *floor* (4) next to a *garden* (1-10 = 4).

5. James Monroe: Paying *money* (Monroe) for a *hive* (5) in a *garden* (1-10 = 5).

6. John Quincy Adams: *Adding* (Adams) *quarters* (Quincy) with *sticks* (6) in a *garden* (1-10 = 6).

7. Andrew Jackson: Playing *jacks* (Jackson) in a *heavenly* (7) *garden* (1-10 = 7).

8. Martin Van Buren: A moving *van* (Van Buren) at a *gate* (8) near a *garden* (1-10 = 8).

9. William Harrison: A *hare* (Harrison) reading a *will* (William) attached to *vines* (9) in a *garden* (1-10 = 9).

10. John Tyler: A *hen* (10) wearing a *tie* (Tyler) in a *garden* (1-10 = 10).

11. James Polk: People in *polka dot* (Polk) outfits eating *buns* (1) on a *summer beach* (second decade: 11-20 = 11).

12. Zachary Taylor: A *tailor* (Taylor) mending a *shoe* (2) on a *summer beach* (11-20 = 12).

13. Millard Fillmore: *Film* (Fillmore) stuck in a *tree* (3) on a *beach* (11-20 = 13).

14. Franklin Pierce: *Piercing* (Pierce) a *floor* (4) on a *beach* (11-20 = 14) with a beach umbrella.

15. James Buchanan: A *cannon* (Buchanan) shooting at *hives* (5) on a *beach* (11-20 = 15).

16. Abraham Lincoln: Toasting sausage *links* (Lincoln) on *sticks* (6) on a *beach* (11-20 = 16).

17. Andrew Johnson: *Ants* (Andrew) crossing a *lawn* (Johnson) in *heavenly* (7) *beach* (11-20 = 17).

18. Ulysses S. Grant: A *grandpa* (Grant) opening a *gate* (8) to a *beach* (11-20 = 18).

19. Rutherford B. Hayes: *Hay* (Hayes) stacks tied up in *vines* (9) on a *beach* (11-20 = 19).

20. James A. Garfield: A *hen* (10) driving a *car* (Garfield) on a *beach* (11-20 = 20).

21. Chester A. Arthur: An *artist* (Arthur) painting people eating *buns* (1) at a *fall Thanksgiving Dinner* scene (third decade: 21-30 = 21).

22. Grover Cleveland: *Leaves* (Cleveland) covering the *shoes* (2) of people at a *fall Thanksgiving Dinner* table (21-30 = 22).

23. Benjamin Harrison: A *hare* (Harrison) playing a *banjo* (Benjamin) in a *tree* (three) to entertain a *Thanksgiving Dinner* scene (21-30 = 23).

24. William McKinley: Someone dropping *macaroni* (McKinley) on the *floor* (4) of a *Thanksgiving Dinner* scene (21-30 = 24).

25. Theodore Roosevelt: *Teddy bears* (Theodore) putting *roses* (Roosevelt) on the *Thanksgiving Dinner* (21-30) table, and swatting at bees from a nearby *hive* (5 = 25).

26. William H. Taft: People pulling *taffy* (Taft) with *sticks* at a *Thanksgiving Dinner*.

27. Woodrow Wilson: Angels in *heaven* (7) getting water from a *well* (Wilson) for a *Thanksgiving Dinner* (21-30 = 27).

28. Warren Harding: Someone leaning on a *gate* (8) with *heartburn* (Harding) from eating too much at a *Thanksgiving Dinner* (21-30 = 28).

29. Calvin Coolidge: A *cooler* (Coolidge) held together with *vines* (9) for a *Thanksgiving Dinner* scene (21-30 = 29).

30. Herbert Hoover: A *hen* cleaning up with a *"hoover"* (Hoover) vacuum cleaner after a *Thanksgiving Dinner* (21-30 = 30).

31. Franklin Roosevelt: A *Franklin stove* (Franklin) warming people who are eating *buns* (1) and putting *roses* (Roosevelt) on a *winter snowman* (4th decade: 31-40 = 31).

32. Harry Truman: A *winter snowman* (31-40) wearing *shoes* (2 = 32) and blowing a *trumpet* (Truman).

33. Dwight Eisenhower: *Ice* (Eisenhower) dripping off a *tree* (3) onto a *snowman* (31-40 = 33).

34. John F. Kennedy: A *can of peas* (Kennedy) eaten by a *winter snowman* (31-40), and spilling on the *floor* (4 = 34).

35. Lyndon B. Johnson: *Lizards* (Lyndon) dropping out of a *hive* (5) held by a *snowman* (31-40 = 35) and crawling across a *lawn* (Johnson).

36. Richard Nixon: A *snowman* (31-40) doing *tricks* (Nixon) with *sticks* (6 = 36).

37. Gerald Ford: A *snowman* (31-40) driving a *Ford car* (Ford) in *heaven* (7 = 37).

38. Jimmy Carter: Someone pushing a *snowman* (31-40) in a *cart* (Carter) through a *gate* (8 = 38).

39. Ronald Reagan: A *snowman* (31-40) shooting a *ray gun* (Reagan) at *vines* (9 = 39).

40. George Bush: A *hen* (10) breaking off pieces of a *bush* (Bush) to use for arms for a *snowman* (31-40 = 40).

World War I

1. *Information:* In 1914 when World War I was just beginning in Europe, there were two major alliance systems. Different groups

of countries in Europe began to form alliances with each other. This means that they agreed not to fight each other, and to defend each other from attacks by countries outside their own alliance system. *Strategy:* The definition of an alliance system needs to be learned. Alliance is an unfamiliar word, therefore an acoustic reconstruction is necessary. Appliance would be a good acoustic reconstruction. A good interactive illustration might be a group of kitchen appliances agreeing not to fight one another, and forming, an "appliance alliance!"

2. *Information:* One of the two major alliance systems in Europe at this time was called the Central Powers. The countries in the Central Powers were: Turkey, Austria-Hungary, and Germany. *Strategy:* The name Central Powers is unfamiliar and must be associated with the names of the particular countries in that alliance system. A good acoustic reconstruction of Central Powers would be Central Park, and a good strategy for remembering the names of the countries would be first letter strategy T-A-G (T=Turkey, A=Austria-Hungary, G=Germany). Then a good elaboration that links the two pieces of information would be a picture of children playing TAG in Central Park.

3. *Information:* The other major alliance system was called the Allied Powers. The countries in the Allied Powers were: France, Italy, Russia, and England. *Strategy:* The name Allied Powers is unfa-

Figure A.2 Countries in the Central Powers (Central Park) = Turkey, Austria-Hungary, and Germany (TAG)

Figure A.3 Countries in the Allied Powers (Allied Van) = France, Italy, Russia, and England (FIRE)

miliar, so a good acoustic reconstruction might be "allied van". Then a good first letter strategy of the names of the countries would be "FIRE" F=France, I=Italy, R=Russia, E=England. Then a good elaboration linking the two pieces of information would be a "FIRE in an Allied Van."

Answers to Chapter 6 Science Exercises

Dinosaurs

The system involves acoustic reconstructions (keywords) for the dinosaur names, symbolic reconstructions for the diet and period attributes, and mimetic (representational) reconstructions for the specific attributes. The diet attribute can be symbolized by coloring the keyword picture *red* for meat-eaters and *green* for plant eaters. The geologic period can be symbolized by showing an *early-morning rooster* (early-Triassic), a *hot, mid-day* sun (middle-Jurassic), or a *late-night owl* (late-Cretaceous). Keywords and mnemonic pictures are provided below:

Name	*Keyword*	*Strategy*
Allosaurus	Aluminum	A *red* box of *aluminum foil* carried in the *hot, mid-day sun,* by a *man running.*

Brachiosaurus	Broccoli	An *enormous green broccoli* in the *hot, mid-day sun*. A man says, "That's the biggest broccoli ever!"
Spinosaurus	Spine	A *late-night owl* putting up a *sail* on a *red spine*.
Coelophysus	Coal	A *red coal* fire in a nursery where *early morning roosters* are *taking care of their young*.
Tyrannosaurus	Tie	*Late-night owls* with *red ties hunting in groups*.
Stegosaurus	Stag	A *green stag* eating *walnuts* in the hot, *mid-day sun*.
Plateosaurus	Plate	An early morning *rooster* carrying *green plates* to a table with *four legs*.
Ankylosaurus	Ankle	A late-night *owl* hitting a *green ankle* with a *club* on its *tail*.

Figure A.4 Brachiosaurus (broccoli) = Ate Plants (green broccoli), Middle Period (mid-day), Biggest Dinosaur (biggest broccoli)

Invertebrate Animals

Two of the names below, earthworm and insect, are very likely to be familiar to students. Therefore, you can use mimetic reconstructions, in which the animal itself, rather than a keyword or symbol, was pictured.

Name	Keyword	Strategy
Mollusk	Mall	People shopping at a *mall* for edible *mollusks*. Mollusks are displayed in store windows as (mimetic) clams and snails.
Arthropods	Artist	An *artist* painting a portrait of *lobsters* and *crabs*.
Insect	(Insect)	*Insects* on *sticks* (pegword for *six*).
Trichina	Trick	A person about to eat an under-cooked roast pig. A *round worm* pops out and says, "I have a *trick*, I'll make you *sick*!"
Earthworm	(Earthworm)	An earthworm coming out of the *earth*, with *many hearts* showing, and a *segmented body*.
Radial Symmetry	Radio Cemetery	A *cemetery* in the shape of a star, with *radios* for headstones. All arms of the star are identical.

Classification of Plants and Animals

Since this is ordered information, the pegword system can be employed. A first letter strategy, in which the first letters of the classification scheme formed the first letters of a memorable sentence, is also possible, (e.g.,"King Phillip came over from Germany Sunday").

Name	Keyword	Number	Pegword	Strategy
Kingdom	King	1	bun	A *king* eating a *bun*.
Phylum	File	2	shoe	A *file* filing a *shoe*.
Class	Class	3	tree	A *class* of school children studying *trees*.

Figure A.5 Earthworm = Lives in Earth, Many Hearts, Segmented Body

Order	Order	4	door	Someone *ordering* a *door* to open.
Family	Family	5	hive	A *family* of bees in a *hive*.
Genus	genius	6	sticks	A *genius* working out a difficult math problem with *sticks*.
Species	spectacles	7	heaven	Angels in *heaven* wearing *spectacles*.

Picturing all these elaborations within a life sciences lab will help retrieve that these are life science classifications.

Earth History

All the following are relatively straightforward keyword strategies, with the exception of *meso-*. "Meso" sounds sufficiently like "middle" so that a person can be shown standing in the middle of the picture and saying, "the meso is the middle."

Name	Keyword	Meaning	Strategy
Paleo-	pail	old	*old* people carrying *pails*
-ology	owl	study of	an *owl studying*
zoo-	zoo	animals	*animals* in a *zoo*
meso-	middle	middle	"the *meso* is the *middle*".
ceno-	cent	new	a machine making *new cents*.

For the attributes, the keywords "pail,""middle," and "cent," represent the names of the eras, and each of the pictures is shown behind "bars," to represent the keyword "zoo." A description of the pictures follows:

Paleozoic: A picture of high mountains in shallow seas (a sign indicates the seas are shallow). A fish and a plant are represented with a number "1" on them to indicate "first." In the sea are floating some *pails*, to represent the keyword. *Scorpions* are riding in the pails.

Mesozoic: In the *middle* of three "cages" (the end ones are small and unclear) are dinosaurs, some dying off (becoming extinct), and a bird with a number "1" flying overhead.

Cenozoic: A cave man is flipping a <u>cent</u>. A glacier with a penguin on top is present, as is a mastodon, dog, and other mammals.

Figure A.6 Ology (owl) = Study of

Figure A.7 Cenozoic (cent) Era = Mammals, Humans, Ice Age

Geology

Minerals:

Name	*Keyword*	*Strategy*
Talc	Tail	A *white tail* with a *bun* on it being powdered.
Crocoite	Crocodile	An *orange* crocodile wearing *shoes* in a *display case*.
Calcite	Cow	A *gray cow* in a *steel tree*.
Wolframite	Wolf	A *black wolf* standing on a *floor* illuminated by *light bulbs*.
Apatite	Ape	A *brown ape* pouring *fertilizer* on a *bee*
Pyrite	Pie	A *yellow pie* on *sticks* with *acid* being poured on it.
Quartz	Quarter	Angels in *heaven* putting *pink quarters* into a *radio*.

Beryl	Barrel	A "metal mixer" (we thought "alloy" would be unfamiliar) pouring "mixed metals" through a *gate* into *green barrels*.
Corundum	Car	A *red car* driving into a clothes *line* on which are hung pieces of *jewelry*.

Type of rock	Examples	Keywords	Strategy
Igneous	basalt granite olivine	salt granny Olive Oyl	A *granny* and *Olive Oyl* at dinner eating a *pig* (igneous). *Granny* is passing the *salt*.
Metamorphic	marble quartz slate	marbles quarts skate	A *dwarf* on *skates* is shooting *marbles* at *quart* bottles.
Sedimentary	sandstone limestone shale*	sand lime nail	*Sand*, *limes*, and *nails* are settling to form sedimentary rock.

*It seems that "*shell*" would be an excellent keyword for "shale." Shell was not used in this case, because shells in fact, having settled, broken

Figure A.8 Types of Metamorphic (dwarf) Rocks = Slate (skate), Marble (marble), Quartz (quarts)

down and solidified, are an important component of *limestone*, and some possibility for confusion may therefore be created.

Answers to Chapter 7 Exercises

Spelling

Spelling Word	Strategy
answer	<u>WE</u> will ans<u>WE</u>r.
believe	I be<u>LIE</u>ve you won't <u>LIE</u>
break	The bird will Br<u>EAK</u> its B<u>EAK</u>.
business	It is a <u>SIN</u> to cheat at bu<u>SIN</u>ess.
does	<u>DO</u> as she <u>DO</u>es.
forty	Here's <u>FOR</u>ty dollars <u>FOR</u> you.
grammar	Bad gram<u>MAR</u> will <u>MAR</u> your speech.
minute	I can crack a <u>NUT</u> in a mi<u>NUT</u>e
none	<u>NONE</u> stands for <u>NO</u> o<u>NE</u>.
piece	Have a <u>PIE</u>ce of <u>PIE</u>.
Wednesday	They will <u>WED</u> on <u>WED</u>nesday.
whole	<u>WHO</u> ate the <u>WHO</u>le pie?
women	<u>WO</u>n't <u>MEN</u> understand <u>WOMEN</u>?

Multiplication

Fact	Strategy
3 X 3 = 9	A *tree* and a *tree* holding up a *line*.
3 X 4 = 12	A *tree* with a *door*. Inside is an *elf*.
3 X 6 = 18	A *sick tree* with *sticks*. An ambulance is *aiding*.
3 X 7 = 21	A *tree* in *heaven*, holding up *twin buns*.
3 X 8 = 24	A *tree* behind a *gate*, with *twin doors*.
4 X 4 = 16	A *door* and a (different) *door*. Someone is *sitting* on them.
4 X 6 = 24	A *door* made of *sticks*, inside are *twin doors*.
4 X 7 = 28	A *door* in *heaven*. Inside are *twin* (pearly?) *gates*.

4 X 8 = 32   Someone kicking a *door* and a *gate* with a *dirty shoe*.

6 X 6 = 36   *Sticks, sticks,* and *dirty sticks.*

6 X 7 = 42   *Sticks* in *heaven,* holding up a *warty shoe.*

6 X 8 = 48   *Sticks* on a *gate,* next to a *warty gate.*

7 X 7 = 49   A cloud (*heaven*) and a different cloud (*heaven*), held together by a *warty line.*

7 X 8 = 56   *Heaven's gate,* inside are *gifty sticks.*

8 X 8 = 64   A *gate* and a *(different) gate,* leading to a *witchy door* (a door with a witch's face).

Students should learn to recite these quickly, as well as recall the picture, such as, "Sticks in heaven, warty shoe: six times seven, forty-two. Door and gate, dirty shoe: four times eight, thirty-two." Also, be careful to discriminate between *pairs,* when they occur (as in 4 X 4; door and *different* door), from *twins* (twenty-four; *twin* doors).

Index